THE
CONSTITUTION
OF THE
UNITED STATES

THE
CONSTITUTION
OF THE
UNITED STATES

Introduction by
EDWARD C. SMITH

Notes and Charts by
WILLIAM R. BARNES

Self-Scoring Examination by
SAMUEL SMITH

BARNES & NOBLE
Booksellers & Publishers
New York

CONTENTS

CHARTS AND TABLES

THE ORIGINS OF THE CONSTITUTION

The Constitution of 1787 was the product of seven centuries of development in England and America. Magna Charta (1215) is as much the heritage of Americans as of Englishmen. So is the common law which limited the authority of the King's ministers as well as governed the King's subjects. The rights and privileges of Parliament were claimed by colonial legislatures against royal governors. From experience in living under charters in some of the colonies, Americans learned the value of written documents which explicitly stated the rights of the people and the government's powers. They were constantly trying to adapt English institutions to the conditions of a new continent and a relatively classless society.

The breach between England and the Americans resulted from their diametrically opposed ideas as to the proper political relationship of the colonies to the mother country. King George III, his ministers, and majorities in Parliament regarded the colonies as subordinate to England. The Americans regarded each colony as a coequal part of the King's dominions and, as such, entitled to self-government and exemption from parliamentary taxation and legislation, and administrative interference. They sought redress of grievances by protests, petitions, nonimportation agreements, and, at last, by resorting to arms.

In May, 1775, three weeks after the Revolutionary War began at Lexington and Concord, the Second Continental Congress met at Philadelphia. It was a revolutionary body deriving its authority from other revolutionary bodies. Its members were delegates of patriotic organizations in each of the colonies sent to concert measures for the common defense. Congress assumed many of the powers of government; it created an army and navy, appointed officers, borrowed money, issued paper currency, and sought help from Europe. It adopted the Declaration of Independence, recommended the creation of state constitutions, and drew up the Articles of Confederation, all highly important in American constitutional development.

THE DECLARATION OF INDEPENDENCE

Though a few radical leaders advocated independence from the beginning, most Americans hoped for eventual reconciliation with

Great Britain. The Congress, on July 6, 1775, issued a lengthy "Declaration of the Causes and Necessity of Taking up Arms," detailing American grievances but explicitly denying an intention to separate from Great Britain and establish independent states. King George replied by proclaiming a state of rebellion in the colonies, and Parliament dutifully passed an act cutting off colonial trade. Moderate leaders now became convinced that independence was the only alternative to submission. Thomas Paine's emotion-charged pamphlet, *Common Sense*, was heavily circulated throughout the colonies and converted thousands of ordinary Americans to the cause of independence. On June 6, 1776, Richard Henry Lee of Virginia proposed the following to the Continental Congress:

> *Resolved*, That these United Colonies are, and of right ought to be, free and independent States, that they are absolved from all allegiance to the British Crown, and that all political connection between them and the State of Great Britain is, and ought to be totally dissolved.

Drafting the Declaration. On June 10 Congress appointed its five most able members—John Adams, Benjamin Franklin, Thomas Jefferson, Robert R. Livingston, and Roger Sherman—as a committee to draft the Declaration. Jefferson was chief author of the draft that was submitted to Congress on June 23. Congress made two or three changes and voted independence on July 2. On July 4 the engrossed copy was signed by John Hancock, President of the Congress. All but one of the other signatures were appended on August 2.

Contents of the Declaration. The underlying philosophy of the Declaration of Independence was derived from John Locke's second treatise *On Civil Government* (1690), which had been written with the avowed purpose of justifying the English Revolution of 1688. According to Locke, men had once lived unrelated lives in a state of nature. At a certain stage of development they entered into a social contract with one another thereby creating both a society and a government. By the terms of the contract each individual surrendered part of his natural rights, and in return received protection and other advantages of organized government. The acts of government must be in accordance with moral principles, what is right or wrong being determined by the will of the majority. If a government seriously threatens the interests of society, the people may pull it down and substitute another government for it. Jefferson omitted a specific reference to the imaginary state of nature and social contract, and asserted that the natural equality of men and their natural rights are "self-evident."

The main body of the Declaration contains twenty-six indictments against the King and Parliament for usurpations and tyrannical acts, such as "abolishing our most valuable laws," and "waging war against us." For these reasons, in the name of the people, the United Colonies were declared free and independent states with all the powers rightfully belonging to sovereign states.

Effects of the Declaration. The Declaration of Independence was a powerful stimulus to the patriot cause. It was both a brilliant justification for resort to arms and an implied promise that American successor governments would be founded on the will of the people. Though it did not immediately result in the emancipation of slaves or in universal suffrage, advocates of both abolition of slavery and suffrage extension in later generations effectively used the equalitarian principles of the Declaration to advance their causes. In our own day it is a prod to the consciences of the American people to improve their treatment of minority groups.

STATE CONSTITUTIONS

Before the end of 1776, conventions or congresses in most states formulated state constitutions, some of which became effective only after being submitted to the voters for approval. These state constitutions faithfully reflected the prevailing ideas of the Revolution concerning the relations between government and people.

Popular Sovereignty and Limited Government. Principles of popular sovereignty and social contract were common to all the constitutions, and were best expressed in the Massachusetts Bill of Rights: "The whole people covenants with each citizen, and each citizen with the whole people that all shall be governed by certain laws for the common good." Most of the constitutions were prefaced by bills of rights which withheld certain powers from the government, limited the government in the exercise of other powers, and provided protection for individuals. The justly famous Virginia Bill of Rights, written by George Mason, became the model for expressions of democratic principles and for later bills of rights in America and Continental Europe.

The Eclipse of the Executive. The King and royal governors were unpopular in 1776, so executive power went into a temporary eclipse. The first constitution of Pennsylvania did not provide for a governor. In ten states the governor's term was only one year, his administrative powers were few, and he was dependent on the legislature. Only New York gave the governor sufficient power and a long enough term (three years) to make him truly the head of the executive branch.

Legislative Supremacy. In a majority of the states the legislature elected the governor, judges, and other officers and determined the policies of government. It possessed lawmaking, financial, and supervisory powers granted in general terms. As the successor of Parliament, it was considered to hold the general residual authority in government, and therefore could exercise any power not granted to another authority. Except in Pennsylvania and Georgia, the legislature was composed of two houses. Members were chosen by voters who in most states were required to own a considerable amount of property.

THE ARTICLES OF CONFEDERATION

The same Virginia resolution that proposed independence called upon Congress to prepare a plan for confederation of the states. On July 12, 1776 debate began on a draft written by John Dickinson, and continued at intervals whenever time could be spared from urgent military matters. It soon became apparent that selfish concerns of the states outweighed considerations of national interest. States with claims to western lands refused to grant Congress power to settle boundary disputes. The small states insisted on amendments to secure their sovereignty. The large states tried (in vain) to apportion voting strength in Congress according to population or the amount that each state contributed to the common fund. The Southern states insisted that expenses of the Confederation should be apportioned according to the value of land in private hands rather than according to total population including slaves. It was not until November 1, 1777 that Congress submitted the Articles to the states for ratification.

Most of the states ratified fairly promptly, but Maryland, expressing fears for her future among powerful neighbors, held out until other states agreed to cede their western lands to the United States. The Articles became effective on March 1, 1781.

Structure of the Confederation. The Articles variously describe the new arrangement as a "confederacy," as a "firm league of friendship," and as a "perpetual Union." It was less a government than an agency for cooperation among state governments. Each state retained its sovereignty, freedom, and independence. The Articles could be amended only with the unanimous approval of the state legislatures. There was no provision for an executive or a permanent judiciary. The only organ of government was a Congress composed of delegations of from two to seven persons, chosen annually, from each state. Each delegation was paid by the state from which it came, and was subject to recall. Each delegation was entitled to cast one vote, and the approval of nine states was required for any important action. Congress was granted authority over military and foreign affairs and many other subjects, but it lacked the essential powers to control commerce or to raise revenue by taxation. It could apportion needed amounts as "requisitions" upon the states which were then supposed to levy appropriate taxes and remit the proceeds. The authority of Congress could not be directly exerted on individuals.

The Confederation Period. Unsettled economic conditions at the close of the Revolution severely tested both the state governments and the Congress. In some states the legislatures felt compelled to yield to the demands of debtors and issue excessive quantities of paper money or enact "stay laws," or moratoria, postponing the dates when debtors were legally obliged to pay their creditors. In violation of the terms of the Articles, some states imposed tariffs or other trade barriers preventing the free flow of commerce from other states. In varying degrees states failed in their financial obligations to the Confederation. Of a total of $10,000,000 requisitioned by Congress, only $1,500,000 was actually paid; one state paid nothing at all. The public debt of the United States actually increased after the close of the war. Congress was maintaining only a small army, 750 officers and men, for the defense of the United States against Indians and other potential enemies. By the Ordinances of 1785 and 1787, Congress established fundamental and durable policies for the survey of public lands and the government of territories, but was unable to promote much settlement in the Northwest Territory. Though the ablest leaders of the country were engaged in diplomacy, they were singularly unsuccessful in negotiating commercial treaties, in part because foreign nations feared that the states would not fulfill the treaty obligations of the United States.

Failure of the Amending Process. In 1781 Congress proposed an amendment to the Articles which would have enabled it to levy a duty of five per cent on all imported goods. All the states ratified the amendment except Rhode Island. A second amendment designed to meet Rhode Island's objections was ratified by twelve states, but this time it was New York that refused to give its approval despite the warning of Congress that without revenues the Confederation would disintegrate. Both Rhode Island and New York possessed fine harbors which served as ports of entry for the trade of nearby states, and both were unwilling to concede any considerable part of the tariff duties for the common good. The attitude of the dominant political groups in these states made it plain that, if the Union were to be strengthened, it must be done by some means other than the cumbrous procedure required by the Articles.

THE MOVEMENT FOR A NEW CONSTITUTION

A number of groups combined in an effort to create the Constitution of the United States. Among the most important were former officers of the Continental Army and former members of Congress who, in the course of their service, had developed national loyalties; leaders from the large states of Virginia, Pennsylvania, and Massachusetts who believed that the ability of one state to veto progress endangered the future of all the states; leaders from the small states of Connecticut, New Jersey, and Delaware who desired relief from the commercial restrictions of New York and Pennsylvania; Georgians who wanted national help against a threatened Indian war; and merchants and ship-owners in all the states. The most active leaders of the movement were Alexander Hamilton of New York who, as military secretary to Washington, had observed the weakness and incapacity of Congress; and James Madison, an ardent nationalist, associate of Jefferson, and opponent of Patrick Henry in Virginia politics.

The Call for the Convention. In 1785 commissioners from Virginia and Maryland settled amicably many disputed points concerning boundaries, navigation in the Chesapeake Bay, and tariff duties. When the Maryland commissioners proposed a larger conference to include Delaware and Pennsylvania, the Virginia legislature seized the opportunity to call a meeting of delegates from all the states at Annapolis in September, 1786. Nine states responded by appointing delegates, but only five states were represented when the conference met. Those present adopted a strongly worded report, supposed to have been written by Hamilton, stressing the deficiencies in the existing government of the United States and calling a convention of all the states to meet in Philadelphia, May 14, 1787, for the purpose of "digesting a Plan" for remedying the defects of the Articles of Confederation. After several states had chosen delegates, Congress issued a formal call for a convention "for the sole and express purpose of revising the Articles of Confederation."

The Selection of Delegates. The Virginia legislature selected an able delegation including Washington, who was prevailed upon to come out of retirement and throw the weight of his influence in favor of the movement, James Madison, George Mason, and Governor Edmund Randolph. The Pennsylvania delegation was the largest, including Franklin, whose reputation was second only to that of Washington; James Wilson, who had consistently expressed the belief that the Americans were one people; and Gouverneur Morris, a brilliant New Yorker temporarily residing in Philadelphia. The New York legislature designated Hamilton but took care to send with him John Lansing and Robert Yates, members of the dominant antifederalist party in the state. The New Hampshire legislature chose delegates but neglected to provide for their expenses; they arrived in late July—after Lansing and Yates of the New York delegation had withdrawn from the convention. Rhode Island alone appointed no delegates, and was unrepresented throughout the deliberations. Other delegates of outstanding abilities were Rufus King and Elbridge Gerry of Massachusetts, Roger Sherman and William Samuel Johnson of Connecticut, and John Rutledge and the two Pinckneys of South Carolina.

Of the fifty-five delegates who attended the convention, thirty-nine had served in Congress, and all were experienced in the politics of their states. A large number of the delegates were young men in their early thirties; the average age was about forty-three. Among those who did not attend the convention were Jefferson and John Adams who were abroad as ministers to France and Great Britain respectively. Patrick Henry and a number of other leaders whose interests were primarily in state politics declined to serve.

THE CONVENTION OF 1787

Only the Virginia and Pennsylvania delegations were in Philadelphia at the appointed time, and it was not until May 25 that the Convention could be organized for business. The delegates unanimously elected Washington as presiding officer. Rules of procedure provided that each state delegation should have one vote. The delegates agreed to keep their deliberations absolutely secret, an action that is partly responsible for the theory—now generally discredited—that they engaged in an undemocratic conspiracy to undo the work of the Revolution. The rule of secrecy enabled the members to express opinions freely and without reserve, to advance tentative proposals, to reconsider decisions without being publicly ridiculed for inconsistency, to compromise, and to concede points in return for intangible advantages. They determined to prepare a comprehensive document and be judged on their work as a whole.

Records of the Convention. Madison, sensing the historical importance of the Convention, obtained its permission to take copious notes on the debates. Other members sometimes helped by giving him copies or outlines of their remarks. Madison's notes, which became available to the public only after his death in 1836, constitute practically the only dependable source of information concerning the debates. In some matters they were supplemented by the recollections of other delegates written after the Convention had adjourned.

The Virginia Plan. After their arrival in Philadelphia, the Virginia delegation drafted a series of resolutions to serve, instead of the Articles of Confederation, as a basis for the discussions. The plan provided for the supremacy of the legislative branch, a national executive, and a system of national courts. The legislature should consist of two houses, one of which should be elected by popular vote, and the other selected by the first house from persons nominated by the state legislatures. A state's voting strength in each house should be in proportion to the amounts contributed by the state or to the number of its free inhabitants. The legislature should have power to enact laws in all cases to which the separate states were incompetent; to disallow states laws contravening the constitution; to call forth the forces of the Union against any recalcitrant state; and to elect the national executive and the judges of national courts.

The delegates debated the Virginia plan for two weeks, making a number of changes. It was agreed that representatives in the lower house should be apportioned according to population, and also—by a margin of one vote—that the same apportionment apply to the second house. The delegation from New Jersey requested an adjournment in order to prepare a different plan.

The New Jersey Plan. On June 15 William Paterson of the New Jersey delegation introduced resolutions that the Convention should confine itself to proposing amendments to the Articles of Confederation as Congress had specified. It suggested that Congress should be granted power to levy duties on foreign goods imported into the United States, to impose a stamp tax on documents, and to regulate the collection of both. If additional revenue was needed, Congress could not only requisition the states, but direct the collection of taxes in noncomplying states. Congress should have power to regulate foreign and interstate commerce. All laws of Congress and all treaties made under the authority of the United States should be the supreme law of the respective states. There was to be a plural executive chosen by Congress, with general authority to execute federal acts, appoint federal officers, and direct all military operations. There was to be a supreme court appointed by the executive with jurisdiction on appeal over cases arising from the construction of treaties, the acts for the regulation of trade, and the collection of revenue.

If the New Jersey plan had been formulated before the Convention met, it would have been satisfactory to all but the most advanced nationalists. As it was, it received the support of New York and Delaware only. But it became obvious that many of the proposals of the Viriginia plan, in particular the apportionment of the upper house according to population, would have to be reconsidered if the support of the small states was to be won.

The Great Compromise. At this point the lines between the large and small states became tightly drawn, and there was talk of breaking up the Convention. The delegates from large states refused to yield on the principle of representation in proportion to population; the small states feared to enter a union completely dominated by the large states. Besides, they argued, the people would never accept a constitution that did not preserve the principle of state equality. After three weeks of recriminations, the delegates agreed to the Great (sometimes called the Connecticut) Compromise: the lower house should be chosen according to population and should have the sole authority to originate revenue bills; and each state would have an equal vote in the upper house.

Compromise of Sectional Interests. Northern commercial interests were anxious for Congress to have power to regulate commerce, and delegates had willingly conceded to the South that no export duties could be levied. In addition to free exportation of their staple crops, the Southerners demanded that Congress be denied power to interfere with the slave trade. The compromise finally arrived at provided, in return for the commerce power, that the slave trade might continue until 1808 with a duty of not more than $10 for each slave imported.

The formula for counting three-fifths of the slaves in apportioning representatives and direct taxes was carried over from one of the unsuccessful amendments previously proposed by Congress.

The Powers of Congress. One by one the broad general grants of power in the Virginia plan were found to be impractical. To disallow state laws would cause resentment, and to use military force was practically equivalent to making war on a state. The delegates decided to enumerate the specific powers which Congress might exercise. The Committee on Detail compiled a list, taking most of the powers—some of them verbatim—from the Articles of Confederation; and others from various state constitutions. From this list the Convention chose many provisions to be included in the Constitution. The taxing power was granted in broad terms, practically unrestrained except as to direct taxes. The necessary-and-proper clause at the end of the enumerated powers gave Congress a choice of means in carrying out the powers of the federal government.

The Executive Article. Nothing gave the Convention so much trouble as the problem of how to create an executive with adequate powers and yet with requisite responsibility to the people. The delegates debated the merits of a plural, as against a single, executive, and considered tenure for life and for seven years without re-eligibility before settling on a four-year term with re-eligibility. In provisions borrowed from the constitution of New York, the Convention created a strong executive; but they made him subject to impeachment and trial by the houses of Congress. As to the method of choosing the President, the Convention discarded legislative election because it would make the President subservient to Congress; and popular election, because it would give excessive influence to the large states. The final solution was the electoral college which was heavily weighted in favor of the small states. The least populous state would have three electors, and a state with ten times as many people would only have four times as many electors. If no candidate received a majority of the electoral college vote, the House of Representatives, voting by states and with each state having one vote, would select from among the five highest candidates. It was expected that Washington would be the first President and would serve as long as he cared to. After that, it was thought the electoral vote would be scattered among celebrities in different states, and the election would be thrown into the House where the small states, being in the majority, would, in fact, choose the President.

The Judiciary Article. The Convention early agreed that there should be a supreme court and that all federal judges should have tenure during good behavior. Sharp differences of opinion arose over whether to create a separate system of lower federal courts or to provide for the trial of federal cases in existing state courts. Without settling the issue, the Convention got it out of the way by providing that Congress might create inferior federal courts. But the Supreme Court was given original jurisdiction to decide cases involving foreign diplomatic and consular officers and disputes between states. Federal judges were to be appointed by the President with the consent of the Senate.

The Supremacy Clause. In Article VI, a provision which had first appeared in the New Jersey plan declared that the Constitution and all laws made in accordance with it, and all treaties, past and future, should be the supreme law of the land. All state judges were bound to uphold the supremacy of valid federal laws and treaties, even if they were in conflict with state constitutions or state laws. Another clause designed to strengthen the Union required all state legislative, executive and judicial officers to take an oath to support the Constitution of the United States.

The Position of States under the Constitution. The federal government was required to guarantee to each state a republican form of government, and to protect it from invasion, and, at its request, from domestic violence. No state, without its own consent, could be divided, or joined with another state, or be deprived of its equal vote in the Senate. Nothing was said about state sovereignty. States were forbidden to coin money, issue paper money, make anything but gold and silver coin a legal tender in payment of debts, pass any law impairing the obligation of contracts, levy taxes on imports or exports, or, without the consent of Congress, enter into a compact with another state. These prohibitions summed up the criticisms of the financial and business community against measures passed by several state legislatures during the confederation period. In order to promote harmonious relations with each other, states were required to give full faith and credit to acts and records of other states, to treat citizens of other states like their own citizens, and to return fugitives from justice and runaway slaves to the states from which they had fled.

Democratic Basis of the Constitution. The preamble of the Articles of Confederation had named all the states in order from north to south. How was the Convention to enumerate the participating states without knowing which would ratify? In a brilliant flash of inspiration, the Convention began with the words, "We the People of the United States . . . do ordain and establish this Constitution. . . ."

The Method of Ratification. The members apparently believed that ratification by state conventions specially elected by the people for the purpose was more democratic than ratification by state legislatures. Besides, as some delegates pointed out, the legislatures would

be prejudiced against an instrument of government that would reduce their own powers. In view of the continued stubbornness of
New York and Rhode Island, the Convention abandoned all thought
of requiring ratification by every state. Allowing for some antifederalist opinion known to exist elsewhere, it voted that the Constitution should go into effect as soon as nine states had ratified.
(Apparently non-ratifying states were to be left to their own resources.)

The Amending Procedure. The delegates were keenly aware that
flaws in the Constitution might appear after it came into operation,
and they were determined not to carry over the disastrous amending
procedure of the Articles. At first they voted that Congress should
call a convention to propose amendments at the request of two-thirds
of the states. To further liberalize the amending procedure they
agreed, toward the end of the session, that two-thirds of both houses
of Congress might also propose amendments. No matter which way
they were proposed, amendments must be ratified either by the
legislatures or by conventions in three-fourths of the states.

Guarantees of Rights. As finally agreed to, the Constitution contained several important guarantees of private rights: the privilege
of habeas corpus and the prohibitions of bills of attainder and ex post
facto laws in Article I, section 9; trial by jury and limitations on trials
for treason in Article III; and a prohibition of religious tests for officers in Article VI. Opinions were expressed that a declaration of
other rights would be superfluous because either they would not be
endangered by federal authorities or would be covered by the common law. Late in the session George Mason and Elbridge Gerry
proposed the appointment of a committee to draft a bill of rights;
the motion failed by a tie vote.

The End of the Session. The provisions already voted were arranged in logical order by a committee on style. Gouverneur Morris
is credited with having written the final draft. Of the fifty-five members who attended the sessions at some time, sixteen had gone home.
Thirty-nine signed the Constitution; Gerry, Mason, and Randolph
for various reasons refused to sign. On September 17, the Convention
adjourned, after having been in practically continuous session for
nearly four months.

Political Theory of the Constitution. Madison and others had
studied the history of previous federations, but fortunately had formulated no hard and fast theories on the subject. Their attitude was

pragmatic. Every provision which they wrote into the Constitution was based on experience in the states, or the colonies, or the mother country. The assignment of power to the federal government was determined by what was needful and what might be acceptable to the state conventions. For theoretical inspiration they leaned heavily on Locke and on Montesquieu's *Spirit of the Laws*. Both writers had insisted on the need for a separation of powers in order to prevent tyranny; in Montesquieu's view even the representatives of the people in the legislature could not be trusted with unlimited power. So they incorporated the power of each branch in a separate article and then devised various checks and balances to compel cooperation among legislative, executive, and judicial branches. There was no mention of a state of nature or an original contract, but by basing the Constitution on the will of the people—as in the preamble and the ratification article—the Convention suggested to persons familiar with Locke's theories a latter-day social contract.

THE CONTEST OVER RATIFICATION

The Convention sent copies of the Constitution to Congress which transmitted them, without comment, to the states. More or less promptly (except in Rhode Island) the legislatures arranged for the selection of delegates to conventions. In the contest over ratification, the federalists, though a minority, had the advantage of unity, initiative, and a novel and interesting proposal. The opposition was divided, overconfident, and badly led.

Discussions in the Press. The text of the Constitution and arguments for and against its adoption occupied much of the space in all American newspapers during the ensuing months. The most noteworthy series of articles in favor of the Constitution was written by Hamilton, Madison, and John Jay for New York newspapers. Out of the terms of the Constitution, they constructed a theory of maximum liberty and governmental effectiveness through federalism; and on theoretical and practical grounds met the objections of the antifederalists. *The Federalist* papers (as the collected articles were later called) remain the best theoretical justification of the American federal system.

The best statement of the antifederalist position was made in a series of "Letters of the Federal Farmer" by Richard Henry Lee. He characterized the new system of government as partly federal but "calculated ultimately to make the states one consolidated government." He warned that adoption of the Constitution would be a fatal

error because the government created under it might abolish the
laws, customs, and constitutions already in existence in America. He
thought the proposed House of Representatives would not be sufficiently responsive to the wishes of the people; and there was no bill
of rights to protect individual liberties. He insisted that the Constitution be amended before, and not after, its adoption by the state
conventions. Other antifederalists, taking a narrow legalistic ap-
proach, argued that the Convention had abused its authority, since
it had been called only to propose amendments to the Articles of
Confederation. They demanded to know by what authority the Convention had used the phrase, "We the People . . . ," since everyone
knew that states were the parties to the compact that had created the
Articles of Confederation. On practical grounds some antifederalists
asserted that a federal government could not effectively exert power
over so large a territory as the United States; others that its capital
would become, as London had been, a center of concentrated power.
Nearly every clause in the proposed constitution was subjected to
adverse criticism.

Ratification of the Constitution. By mid-January, 1788, five state
conventions had ratified—Delaware, New Jersey, and Georgia unanimously, and Connecticut and Pennsylvania by votes of two or three
to one. Maryland approved on April 28 and South Carolina on May
23, by overwhelming majorities. Serious trouble was encountered
in all other states. When the Massachusetts convention had met in
January, preliminary votes showed that a majority of the delegates
was opposed to the Constitution; they were led by Gerry, Samuel
Adams, and John Hancock. After heated discussion, the opposition
weakened, and Massachusetts ratified on February 6. In New Hampshire the federalists avoided defeat in January by procuring a long
adjournment. After a bitter struggle, they won out on June 21, when
New Hampshire became the ninth state to ratify. Four days later,
the Virginia federalists under the leadership of Madison and John
Marshall overcame an early disadvantage, despite the efforts of
George Mason, Patrick Henry, and Richard Henry Lee. In New
York the antifederalists at first had an advantage of two to one; but
when the practical issue became whether to enter the Union or stay
out, the convention ratified by a majority of three votes, July 26, 1788.
The new government began with eleven states in the Union on April
30, 1789. North Carolina entered the Union the following November
and Rhode Island more than a year later.

In the state conventions the principal strength of the federalists
came from representatives of ship-owners, merchants, and handi-

craftsmen in the towns near the Atlantic coast, and of frontiersmen. These groups were apparently convinced of the need for more adequate foreign and military policies and an end to interstate trade barriers. Opposition to the Constitution was strongest among the people in up-country agricultural areas where the principal needs were better roads and courthouse services both of which state and local governments could supply. In varying degrees, antifederalist attitudes were determined by alignments in state and local politics, vague fears of a federal colossus, and the conviction, held especially in New York and Rhode Island, that the establishment of the new federal government would mean increased state and federal taxes on land and other property. In the debates over ratification, the most criticized feature of the Constitution was the lack of a bill of rights. The federalists promised that a bill of rights would be added later through the amendment process. They were not obliged to yield on any other point, but consistently gained support as the discussions in state conventions proceeded.

THE BILL OF RIGHTS

The federalists kept their word. In his first inaugural address, Washington suggested that Congress might initiate the amendment process to meet objections to the Constitution, and Madison, on June 8, 1789, introduced a series of amendments in the House of Representatives. He intended them to be inserted at appropriate places in the text of the Constitution; but Roger Sherman was instrumental in having them appended at the end, where each amendment would stand on its own merits. Nevertheless, they may be regarded as part of the original Constitution.

Substantive Rights. The first three amendments guarantee individual freedom against arbitrary restrictive acts of government. The First prohibits the establishment of a state-supported church, requires the separation of church and state, and guarantees freedom of worship, of speech and of the press, and the rights of peaceable assembly, association, and petition. Though a few Supreme Court justices have held that First Amendment freedoms are absolute or occupy a "preferred position," the Court has usually held that they may be limited so as to protect the rights of others (as from libel) or to guard against clear and present danger of subversion of government or weakening its efforts in war time. The Second and Third Amendments are hedged about with exceptions and relate to subjects that are of little importance today.

Procedural Rights. The next five amendments are concerned mostly with protecting the rights of persons in criminal proceedings, beginning with the gathering of evidence and extending to the imposition of sentences. As interpreted by the courts, they prohibit searches without warrants, wire-tapping, extorted confessions, unduly continued questioning by police, denial of reasonable bail, delayed trials, or trials without indictment, or at places far from the scene of the crime, or juries from which members of the accused's race have been deliberately or systematically excluded, or double jeopardy, or excessive punishments.

An accused person is entitled to be informed of the charges against him, to confront his accusers in open court, and to have the court's help in compelling the attendance of witnesses who may testify in his behalf. He is entitled to consult freely with his lawyers at all stages of the proceedings, and his lawyers must be allowed sufficient time in which to prepare his defense. If he is indigent, the court must provide counsel to defend him. The requirement of due process of law also governs these and other matters including the judge's fairness in conducting the trial.

Explanatory Amendments. The Ninth Amendment was probably intended to reassure the public that the enumeration of certain rights was not intended to exclude the operation of the common law in maintaining others. In Congressional debates on the Tenth Amendment, the antifederalists made a determined but unsuccessful effort to amend so as to confine the federal government to expressly granted powers and to insert the word "thereof" after "people." As the amendment stands, it leaves intact the principle of implied powers and acknowledges the existence of a reservoir of undefined rights belonging to the people of the United States. The Supreme Court has sometimes applied the amendment so as to establish so-called dual federalism, an excessively strict division of powers between the states and the federal government.

VIRGINIA BILL OF RIGHTS *

Adopted June 12, 1776

A declaration of rights made by the representatives of the good people of Virginia, assembled in full and free convention; which rights do pertain to them and their posterity, as the basis and foundation of government.

SECTION 1. That all men are by nature equally free and independent, and have certain inherent rights, of which, when they enter into a state of society, they cannot, by any compact, deprive or divest their posterity; namely, the enjoyment of life and liberty, with the means of acquiring and possessing property, and pursuing and obtaining happiness and safety.

SECTION 2. That all power is vested in, and consequently derived from, the people; that magistrates are their trustees and servants, and at all times amenable to them.

SECTION 3. That government is, or ought to be, instituted for the common benefit, protection, and security of the people, nation, or community; of all the various modes and forms of government, that is best which is capable of producing the greatest degree of happiness and safety, and is most effectually secured against the danger of maladministration; and that, when any government shall be found inadequate or contrary to these purposes, a majority of the community hath an indubitable, inalienable, and indefeasible right to reform, alter, or abolish it, in such manner as shall be judged most conducive to the public weal.

SECTION 4. That no man, or set of men, are entitled to exclusive or separate emoluments or privileges from the community, but in

* B. P. Poore, ed., *The Federal and States Constitutions, Colonial Charters, and other Organic Laws of the United States* (2nd ed., Washington, D.C.: Government Printing Office, 1878), II, 1908 ff.

consideration of public services; which, not being descendible, neither ought the offices of magistrate, legislator, or judge to be hereditary.

SECTION 5. That the legislative and executive powers of the State should be separate and distinct from the judiciary; and that the members of the two first may be restrained from oppression, by feeling and participating the burdens of the people, they should, at fixed periods, be reduced to a private station, return into that body from which they were originally taken, and the vacancies be supplied by frequent, certain, and regular elections, in which all, or any part of the former members, to be again eligible, or ineligible, as the laws shall direct.

SECTION 6. That elections of members to serve as representatives of the people, in assembly, ought to be free; and that all men, having sufficient evidence of permanent common interest with, and attachment to, the community, have the right of suffrage, and cannot be taxed or deprived of their property for public uses, without their own consent, or that of their representatives so elected, nor bound by any law to which they have not, in like manner, assented, for the public good.

SECTION 7. That all power of suspending laws, or the execution of laws, by any authority, without consent of the representatives of the people, is injurious to their rights, and ought not to be exercised.

SECTION 8. That in all capital or criminal prosecutions a man hath a right to demand the cause and nature of his accusation, to be confronted with the accusers and witnesses, to call for evidence in his favor, and to a speedy trial by an impartial jury of twelve men of his vicinage, without whose unanimous consent he cannot be found guilty; nor can he be compelled to give evidence against himself; that no man be deprived of his liberty, except by the law of the land or the judgment of his peers.

SECTION 9. That excessive bail ought not to be required, nor excessive fines imposed, nor cruel and unusual punishment inflicted.

SECTION 10. That general warrants, whereby an officer or messenger may be commanded to search suspected places without evidence of a fact committed, or to seize any person or persons not named, or whose offence is not particularly described and supported by evidence, are grievous and oppressive, and ought not to be granted.

SECTION 11. That in controversies respecting property, and in suits between man and man, the ancient trial by jury is preferable to any other, and ought to be held sacred.

SECTION 12. That the freedom of the press is one of the great bulwarks of liberty, and can never be restrained but by despotic governments.

SECTION 13. That a well-regulated militia, composed of the body of the people, trained to arms, is the proper, natural, and safe defence of a free State; that standing armies, in time of peace, should be avoided, as dangerous to liberty; and that in all cases the military should be under strict subordination to, and governed by, the civil power.

SECTION 14. That the people have a right to uniform government; and, therefore, that no government separate from, or independent of the government of Virginia, ought to be erected or established within the limits thereof.

SECTION 15. That no free government, or the blessings of liberty, can be preserved to any people, but by a firm adherence to justice, moderation, temperance, frugality, and virtue, and by frequent recurrence to fundamental principles.

SECTION 16. That religion, or the duty which we owe to our Creator, and the manner of discharging it, can be directed only by reason and conviction, not by force or violence; and therefore all men are equally entitled to the free exercise of religion, according to the dictates of conscience; and that it is the mutual duty of all to practise Christian forbearance, love, and charity towards each other.

A DECLARATION

BY THE REPRESENTATIVES OF THE UNITED STATES
OF AMERICA IN GENERAL CONGRESS ASSEMBLED

July 4, 1776

WHEN, in the course of human events, it becomes necessary for one people to dissolve the political bands which have connected them with another, and to assume, among the powers of the earth, the separate and equal station to which the laws of nature and of nature's God entitle them, a decent respect to the opinions of mankind requires that they should declare the causes which impel them to the separation.

We hold these truths to be self-evident, that all men are created equal; that they are endowed by their Creator with certain unalienable rights; that among these, are life, liberty, and the pursuit of happiness. That, to secure these rights, governments are instituted among men, deriving their just powers from the consent of the governed; that, whenever any form of government becomes destructive of these ends, it is the right of the people to alter or to abolish it, and to institute a new government, laying its foundation on such principles, and organizing its powers in such form, as to them shall seem most likely to effect their safety and happiness. Prudence, indeed, will dictate that governments long established, should not be changed for light and transient causes; and, accordingly, all experience hath shown, that mankind are more disposed to suffer, while evils are sufferable, than to right themselves by abolishing the forms to which they are accustomed. But, when a long train of abuses and usurpations, pursuing invariably the same object, evinces a design to reduce them under absolute despotism, it is their right, it is their duty, to throw off such government and to provide new guards for their future security. Such has been the patient sufferance of these colonies, and such is now the necessity which constrains them to alter their former systems of government. The history of the present King of Great Britain is a history of repeated injuries and usurpations, all having, in direct object, the establishment of an absolute tyranny over these States. To prove this, let facts be submitted to a candid world:—

He has refused his assent to laws the most wholesome and necessary for the public good.

He has forbidden his governors to pass laws of immediate and pressing importance, unless suspended in their operation till his assent should be obtained; and, when so suspended, he has utterly neglected to attend to them.

He has refused to pass other laws for the accommodation of large districts of people, unless those people would relinquish the right of representation in the legislature: a right inestimable to them, and formidable to tyrants only.

He has called together legislative bodies at places unusual, uncomfortable, and distant from the depository of their public records, for the sole purpose of fatiguing them into compliance with his measures.

He has dissolved representative houses repeatedly for opposing, with manly firmness, his invasions on the rights of the people.

He has refused, for a long time after such dissolutions, to cause others to be elected; whereby the legislative powers, incapable of annihilation, have returned to the people at large for their exercise; the state remaining, in the meantime, exposed to all the danger of invasion from without, and convulsions within.

He has endeavored to prevent the population of these States; for that purpose, obstructing the laws for naturalization of foreigners, refusing to pass others to encourage their migration hither, and raising the conditions of new appropriations of lands.

He has obstructed the administration of justice, by refusing his assent to laws for establishing judiciary powers.

He has made judges dependent on his will alone, for the tenure of their offices, and the amount and payment of their salaries.

He has erected a multitude of new offices, and sent hither swarms of officers, to harass our people, and eat out their substance.

He has kept among us, in time of peace, standing armies, without the consent of our legislatures.

He has affected to render the military independent of, and superior to, the civil power.

He has combined, with others, to subject us to a jurisdiction foreign to our Constitution, and unacknowledged by our laws; giving his assent to their acts of pretended legislation:

For quartering large bodies of armed troops among us:

For protecting them by a mock trial, from punishment, for any murders which they should commit on the inhabitants of these States:

For cutting off our trade with all parts of the world:

For imposing taxes on us without our consent:

For depriving us, in many cases, of the benefit of trial by jury:

For transporting us beyond seas to be tried for pretended offenses:

For abolishing the free system of English laws in a neighboring province, establishing therein an arbitrary government, and enlarging its boundaries, so as to render it at once an example and fit instrument for introducing the same absolute rule into these colonies:

For taking away our charters, abolishing our most valuable laws, and altering, fundamentally, the powers of our governments:

For suspending our own legislatures, and declaring themselves invested with power to legislate for us in all cases whatsoever.

He has abdicated government here, by declaring us out of his protection, and waging war against us.

He has plundered our seas, ravaged our coasts, burnt our towns, and destroyed the lives of our people.

He is, at this time, transporting large armies of foreign mercenaries to complete the works of death, desolation, and tyranny, already begun, with circumstances of cruelty and perfidy scarcely paralleled in the most barbarous ages, and totally unworthy the head of a civilized nation.

He has constrained our fellow citizens, taken captive on the high seas, to bear arms against their country, to become the executioners of their friends, and brethren, or to fall themselves by their hands.

He has excited domestic insurrections amongst us, and has endeavored to bring on the inhabitants of our frontiers, the merciless Indian savages, whose known rule of warfare is an undistinguished destruction of all ages, sexes, and conditions.

In every stage of these oppressions, we have petitioned for redress, in the most humble terms; our repeated petitions have been answered only by repeated injury. A prince, whose character is thus marked by every act which may define a tyrant, is unfit to be the ruler of a free people.

Nor have we been wanting in attention to our British brethren. We have warned them, from time to time, of attempts made by their legislature to extend an unwarrantable jurisdiction over us. We have reminded them of the circumstances of our emigration and settlement here. We have appealed to their native justice and magnanimity, and we have conjured them, by the ties of our common kindred, to disavow these usurpations, which would inevitably interrupt our connections and correspondence. They, too, have been deaf to the voice of justice and consanguinity. We must, therefore, acquiesce in the necessity which denounces our separation, and hold them, as we hold the rest of mankind, enemies in war, in peace, friends.

We, therefore, the representatives of the United States of America, in general Congress assembled, appealing to the Supreme Judge of the world for the rectitude of our intentions, do, in the name, and by the authority of the good people of these colonies, solemnly publish and declare, that these united colonies are, and of right ought to be, free and independent states: that they are absolved from all allegiance to the British Crown, and that all political connection between them and the state of Great Britain is, and ought to be, totally dissolved; and that, as free and independent states, they have full power to levy war, conclude peace, contract alliances, establish commerce, and to do all other acts and things which independent states may of right do. And, for the support of this declaration, with a firm reliance on the protection of Divine Providence, we mutually pledge to each other our lives, our fortunes, and our sacred honor.

ARTICLES OF CONFEDERATION

Adopted November 15, 1777
Ratified and effective March 1, 1781

To all to whom these Presents shall come, we the undersigned Delegates of the States affixed to our Names send greeting.

Whereas the Delegates of the United States of America, in Congress assembled, did, on the fifteenth day of November in the Year of our Lord One Thousand Seven Hundred and Seventy seven, and in the Second Year of the Independence of America, agree to certain articles of Confederation and perpetual Union between the States of Newhampshire, Massachusetts-bay, Rhodeisland and Providence Plantations, Connecticut, New York, New Jersey, Pennsylvania, Delaware, Maryland, Virginia, North-Carolina, South-Carolina, and Georgia in the words following, viz. "Articles of Confederation and perpetual Union between the states of Newhampshire, Massachusetts-bay, Rhodeisland and Providence Plantations, Connecticut, New-York, New-Jersey, Pennsylvania, Delaware, Maryland, Virginia, North-Carolina, South-Carolina and Georgia.

ARTICLE I. The Stile of this Confederacy shall be "The United States of America."

ARTICLE II. Each state retains its sovereignty, freedom, and independence, and every Power, Jurisdiction and right, which is not by this confederation expressly delegated to the United States, in Congress assembled.

ARTICLE III. The said states hereby severally enter into a firm league of friendship with each other, for their common defence, the security of their Liberties, and their mutual and general welfare, binding themselves to assist each other, against all force offered to, or attacks made upon them, or any of them, on account of religion, sovereignty, trade, or any other pretence whatever.

ARTICLE IV. The better to secure and perpetuate mutual friendship and intercourse among the people of the different states in this union, the free inhabitants of each of these states, paupers, vagabonds and fugitives from justice excepted, shall be entitled to all privileges and immunities of free citizens in the several states; and the people of each state shall have free ingress and regress to and from any other state, and shall enjoy therein all the privileges of trade and commerce, subject to the same duties, impositions and restrictions as the inhabitants thereof respectively, provided that such restrictions shall not extend so far as to prevent the removal of property imported into any state, to any other state of which the Owner is an inhabitant; provided also that no imposition, duties or restrictions shall be laid by any state, on the property of the united states, or either of them.

If any Person guilty of, or charged with treason, felony, or other high misdeameanor in any state, shall flee from Justice, and be found in any of the united states, he shall, upon demand of the Governor or executive power, of the state from which he fled, be delivered up and removed to the state having jurisdiction of his offence.

Full faith and credit shall be given in each of these states to the records, acts and judicial proceedings of the courts and magistrates of every other state.

ARTICLE V. For the more convenient management of the general interests of the united states, delegates shall be annually appointed in such manner as the legislature of each state shall direct, to meet in Congress on the first Monday in November, in every year, with a power reserved to each state, to recall its delegates, or any of them, at any time within the year, and to send others in their stead, for the remainder of the Year.

No state shall be represented in Congress by less than two, nor by more than seven Members; and no person shall be capable of being a delegate for more than three years in any term of six years; nor shall any person, being a delegate, be capable of holding any office under the united states, for which he, or another of his benefit receives any salary, fees or emolument of any kind.

Each state shall maintain its own delegates in a meeting of the states, and while they act as members of the committee of the states.

In determining questions in the united states in Congress assembled, each state shall have one vote.

Freedom of speech and debate in Congress shall not be impeached or questioned in any Court, or place out of Congress, and the members of congress shall be protected in their persons from arrests and imprisonments, during the time of their going to and from, and attendance on Congress, except for treason, felony, or breach of the peace.

ARTICLE VI. No state without the Consent of the united states in congress assembled, shall send any embassy to, or receive any embassy from, or enter into any conference, agreement, alliance or treaty with any King, prince or state; nor shall any person holding any office of profit or trust under the united states, or any of them, accept of any present, emolument, office or title of any kind whatever from any king, prince or foreign state; nor shall the united states in congress assembled, or any of them, grant any title of nobility.

No two or more states shall enter into any treaty, confederation or alliance whatever between them, without the consent of the united states in congress assembled, specifying accurately the purposes for which the same is to be entered into, and how long it shall continue.

No state shall lay any imposts or duties, which may interfere with any stipulations in treaties, entered into by the United States in Congress assembled, with any king, prince or state, in pursuance of any treaties already proposed by congress, to the courts of France and Spain.

No vessels of war shall be kept up in time of peace by any state, except such number only, as shall be deemed necessary by the united states in congress assembled, for the defence of such state, or its trade; nor shall any body of forces be kept up by any state, in time of peace, except such number only, as in the judgment of the united states, in congress assembled, shall be deemed requisite to garrison the forts necessary for the defence of such state; but every state shall always keep up a well regulated and disciplined militia, sufficiently armed and accoutred, and shall provide and constantly have ready for use, in public stores, a due number of field pieces and tents, and a proper quantity of arms, ammunition and camp equipage.

No state shall engage in any war without the consent of the united states in congress assembled, unless such state be actually invaded by enemies, or shall have received certain advice of a resolution being formed by some nation of Indians to invade such state, and the danger is so imminent as not to admit of a delay till the united states in congress assembled can be consulted: nor shall any state grant commissions to any ships or vessels of war, nor letters of marque or reprisal, except it be after a declaration of war by the united states in congress assembled, and then only against the kingdom or state and the subjects thereof, against which war has been so declared, and under such regulations as shall be established by the united states in congress assembled, unless such state be infested by pirates, in which case vessels of war may be fitted out for that occasion, and kept so long as the danger shall continue, or until the united states in congress assembled, shall determine otherwise.

ARTICLE VII. When land-forces are raised by any state for the common defence, all officers of or under the rank of colonel, shall be appointed by the legislature of each state respectively, by whom such forces shall be raised, or in such manner as such state shall direct, and all vacancies shall be filled up by the State which first made the appointment.

ARTICLE VIII. All charges of war, and all other expences that shall be incurred for the common defence or general welfare, and allowed by the united states in congress assembled, shall be defrayed out of a common treasury, which shall be supplied by the several states in proportion to the value of all land within each state, granted to or surveyed for any Person, as such land and the buildings and improvements thereon shall be estimated according to such mode as the united states in congress assembled, shall from time to time direct and appoint.

The taxes for paying that proportion shall be laid and levied by the authority and direction of the legislatures of the several states within the time agreed upon by the United States in Congress assembled.

ARTICLE IX. The united states in congress assembled, shall have the sole and exclusive right and power of determining on peace and war, except in the cases mentioned in the sixth article—of sending and receiving ambassadors—entering into treaties and alliances, provided that no treaty of commerce shall be made whereby the legislative power of the respective states shall be restrained from imposing such imposts and duties on foreigners as their own people are subjected to, or from prohibiting the exploration or importation of any species of goods or commodities, whatsoever—of establishing rules for deciding in all cases, what captures on land or water shall be legal, and in what manner prizes taken by land or naval forces in the service of the united states shall be divided or appropriated—of granting letters of marque and reprisal in times of peace—appointing courts for the trial of piracies and felonies committed on the high seas and establishing courts for receiving and determining finally appeals in all cases of captures, provided that no member of congress shall be appointed a judge of any of the said courts.

The united states in congress assembled shall also be the last resort on appeal in all disputes and differences now subsisting or that hereafter may arise between two or more states concerning boundary, jurisdiction or any other cause whatever; which authority shall always be exercised in the manner following. Whenever the legislative or executive authority or lawful agent of any state in controversy with another shall present a petition to congress stating the matter in question and praying for a hearing, notice thereof shall be given by order of congress to the legislative or executive authority of the other state in controversy, and a day assigned for the appearance of the parties by their lawful agents, who shall then be directed to appoint by joint consent, commissioners or judges to constitute a court for hearing and determining the matter in question: but if they cannot agree, congress shall name three persons out of each of the united states, and from the list of such persons each party shall alternately strike out one, the petitioners beginning, until the number shall be reduced to thirteen; and from that number not less than seven, nor more than nine names as congress shall direct, shall in the presence of congress be drawn out by lot, and the persons whose names shall be so drawn or any five of them, shall be commissioners or judges, to hear and finally determine the controversy, so always as a major part of the judges who shall hear the cause shall agree in the determination: and if either party shall neglect to attend at the day appointed, without showing reasons, which congress shall judge sufficient, or being present shall refuse to strike, the congress shall proceed to nominate three persons out of each state, and the secretary of congress shall strike in behalf of such party absent or refusing; and the judgment and sentence of the court to be appointed, in the manner before prescribed, shall be final and conclusive; and if any of the parties shall refuse to submit to the authority of such court, or to appear or defend their claim or cause, the court shall nevertheless proceed to pronounce sentence, or judgment, which shall in like manner be final and decisive, the judgment or sentence and other proceedings being in either case transmitted to congress, and lodged among the acts of congress for the security of the parties concerned: provided that every commissioner, before he sits in judgment, shall take an oath to be administered by one of the judges of the supreme or superior court of the state where the cause shall be tried, "well and truly to hear and determine the matter in question, according to the best of his judgment, without favour, affection or hope of reward:" provided also, that no state shall be deprived of territory for the benefit of the united states.

All controversies concerning the private right of soil claimed under different grants of two or more states, whose jurisdictions as they may respect such lands, and the states which passed such grants are adjusted, the said grants or either of them being at the same time claimed to have originated antecedent to such settlement of jurisdiction, shall on the petition of either party to the congress of the united states, be finally determined as near as may be in the same manner as is before prescribed for deciding disputes respecting territorial juris-diction between different states.

The united states in congress assembled shall also have the sole and exclusive right and power of regulating the alloy and value of coin struck by their own authority, or by that of the respective states—fixing the standard of weights and measures throughout the united states—regulating the trade and managing all affairs with the Indians, not members of any of the states, provided that the legislative right of any state within its own limits be not infringed or violated—establishing and regulating post-offices from one state to another, throughout all the united states, and exacting such postage on the papers passing thro' the same as may be requisite to defray the ex-pences of the said office—appointing all officers of the land forces, in the service of the united states, excepting regimental officers—ap-pointing all the officers of the naval forces, and commissioning all officers whatever in the service of the united states—making rules for the government and regulation of the said land and naval forces, and directing their operations.

The united states in congress assembled shall have authority to appoint a committee, to sit in the recess of congress, to be denomi-nated "A Committee of the States," and to consist of one delegate from each state; and to appoint such other committees and civil officers as may be necessary for managing the general affairs of the united states under their direction—to appoint one of their number to preside, provided that no person be allowed to serve in the office of president more than one year in any term of three years; to ascer-tain the necessary sums of money to be raised for the service of the united states, and to appropriate and apply the same for defraying the public expences—to borrow money, or emit bills on the credit of the united states, transmitting every half year to the respective states an account of the sums of money so borrowed or emitted,—to build and equip a navy—to agree upon the number of land forces, and to make requisitions from each state for its quota, in proportion to the number of white inhabitants in such state; which requisition shall be binding, and thereupon the legislature of each state shall appoint the regimental officers, raise the men and cloath, arm and equip them in a soldier like manner, at the expence of the united states; and the officers and men so cloathed, armed and equipped shall march to the place appointed, and within the time agreed on by the united states in congress assembled: But if the united states in congress assembled shall, on consideration of circumstances judge proper that any state should not raise men, or should raise a smaller number than its quota, and that any other state should raise a greater number of men than the quota thereof, such extra number shall be raised, officered, cloathed, armed and equipped in the same manner as the quota of such state, unless the legislature of such state shall judge that such extra number cannot be safely spared out of the same, in which case they shall raise officer, cloath, arm and equip as many of such extra number as they judge can be safely spared. And the officers and men so cloathed, armed and equipped, shall march to the place appointed, and within the time agreed on by the united states in congress assembled.

The united states in congress assembled shall never engage in a war, nor grant letters of marque and reprisal in time of peace, nor enter into any treaties or alliances, nor coin money, nor regulate the value thereof, nor ascertain the sums and expences necessary for the defence and welfare of the united states, or any of them, nor emit bills, nor borrow money on the credit of the united states, nor appropriate money, nor agree upon the number of vessels of war, to be built or purchased, or the number of land or sea forces to be raised, nor appoint a commander in chief of the army or navy, unless nine states assent to the same: nor shall a question on any other point, except for adjourning from day to day be determined, unless by the votes of a majority of the united states in congress assembled.

The congress of the united states shall have power to adjourn to any time within the year, and to any place within the united states, so that no period of adjournment be for a longer duration than the space of six Months, and shall publish the Journal of their proceedings monthly, except such parts thereof relating to treaties, alliances or military operations, as in their judgment require secrecy; and the yeas and nays of the delegates of each state on any question shall be entered on the Journal, when it is desired by any delegate; and the delegates of a state, or any of them, at his or their request shall be furnished with a transcript of the said Journal, except such parts as are above excepted, to lay before the legislatures of the several states.

ARTICLE X. The committee of the states, or any nine of them, shall be authorized to execute, in the recess of congress, such of the powers of congress as the united states in congress assembled, by the consent of nine states, shall from time to time think expedient to vest them with; provided that no power be delegated to the said committee, for the exercise of which, by the articles of confederation, the voice of nine states in the congress of the united states assembled is requisite.

ARTICLE XI. Canada acceding to this confederation, and joining in the measures of the united states, shall be admitted into, and entitled to all the advantages of this union: but no other colony shall be admitted into the same, unless such admission be agreed to by nine states.

ARTICLE XII. All bills of credit emitted, monies borrowed and debts contracted by, or under the authority of Congress, before the assembling of the united states, in pursuance of the present confederation, shall be deemed and considered as a charge against the united states, for payment and satisfaction whereof the said united states, and the public faith are hereby solemnly pledged.

ARTICLE XIII. Every state shall abide by the determinations of the united states in congress assembled, on all questions which by this confederation are submitted to them. And the Articles of this confederation shall be inviolably observed by every state, and the union shall be perpetual; nor shall any alteration at any time hereafter be made in any of them; unless such alteration be agreed to in a congress of the united states, and be afterwards confirmed by the legislatures of every state.

And Whereas it has pleased the Great Governor of the World to incline the hearts of the legislatures we respectively represent in congress, to approve of, and to authorize us to ratify the said articles of confederation and perpetual union. Know Ye that we the undersigned delegates, by virtue of the power and authority to us given for that purpose, do by these presents, in the name and in behalf of our respective constituents, fully and entirely ratify and confirm each and every of the said articles of confederation and perpetual union, and all and singular the matters and things therein contained: And we do further solemnly plight and engage the faith of our respective constituents, that they shall abide by the determinations of the united states in congress assembled, on all questions, which by the said confederation are submitted to them. And that the articles thereof shall be inviolably observed by the states we respectively represent, and that the union shall be perpetual. In Witness whereof we have hereunto set our hands in Congress. Done at Philadelphia in the state of Pennsylvania the ninth day of July, in the year of our Lord one Thousand seven Hundred and Seventy-eight, and in the third year of the independence of America. [Names omitted]

SOME PRESIDENTIAL OPINIONS CONCERNING
THE CONSTITUTION

"If, in the opinion of the people, the distribution or modification of the Constitutional powers be in any particular wrong, let it be corrected by an amendment in the way in which the Constitution designates. But let there be no change by usurpation; for although this, in one instance, may be the instrument of good, it is the customary weapon by which free governments are destroyed."

—GEORGE WASHINGTON

"It would be a dangerous delusion if our confidence in the men of our choice should silence our fears for the safety of our rights. Confidence is everywhere the parent of despotism. Free government is founded on jealousy, not in confidence. It is jealousy and not confidence which prescribes limited constitutions to bind down those whom we are obliged to trust with power. Our Constitution has accordingly fixed the limits to which, and no further, our confidence will go. In questions of power, then, let no more be heard of confidence in man, but bind him down from mischief by the chains of the Constitution."

—THOMAS JEFFERSON

"There is even now something of ill omen among us. I mean the increasing disregard for law which pervades the country; the growing disposition to substitute wild and furious passions in lieu of the sober judgments of courts. . . . As the patriots of seventy-six did to the support of the Declaration of Independence, so to the support of the Constitution and Laws let every American pledge his life, property, and his sacred honor; let every man remember that to violate the law is to trample on the blood of his father, and to tear the charter of his own and his children's liberty."

—ABRAHAM LINCOLN

"It may be the highest duty of a judge at any given moment to disregard, not merely the wishes of individuals of great political or financial power, but the overwhelming tide of public sentiment; and the judge who does thus disregard public sentiment when it is wrong, who brushes aside the plea of any special interest when the plea is not founded on righteousness, performs the highest service to the country."

—THEODORE ROOSEVELT

"This method of uniting popular control with self-imposed restraint through a Constitution and an independent Judiciary to enforce it, is the secret of the strength of our Nation, and it explains why we have lived and grown stronger under the same Constitution, in the face of all kinds of obstacles, including the greatest civil war in history, and the difficulties of a material expansion and growth of population beyond the dreams of the most imaginative statesmen."

—WILLIAM H. TAFT

"The men who framed the federal Constitution were also practical statesmen with an experienced eye for affairs and a quick practical sagacity in respect of the actual structure of government, and they have given us a thoroughly workable model. If it had in fact been a machine governed by mechanically automatic balances, it would have had no history; but it was not, and its history has been rich with the influences and personalities of the men who have conducted it and made it a living reality. The government of the United States has had a vital and normal organic growth and has proved itself eminently adapted to express the changing temper and purposes of the American people from age to age."

—WOODROW WILSON

"The Constitution is the sole source and guaranty of national freedom. We believe that the safest place to declare and interpret the Constitution which the people have made is the Supreme Court of the United States."

—CALVIN COOLIDGE

"It was the spirit of liberty which made our American civilization. That spirit made the Constitution. If that spirit is gone the Constitution is gone, even though its words remain. . . Whatever that change may be, it must be clear of those confusions which impair the great safeguards of human liberty. There must never be confusion in the Bill of Rights, the balance of power, local government, and a government of laws, not of men."

—HERBERT HOOVER

"Our Constitution is so simple, so practical that it is possible always to meet extraordinary needs by changes in emphasis and arrangement without loss of essential form. That is why our constitutional system has proved itself the most superbly enduring political mechanism the world has ever seen. It has met every stress of vast expansion of territory, of foreign wars, of bitter internal strife, of world relations."

—FRANKLIN D. ROOSEVELT

THE GOVERNMENT OF THE UNITED STATES

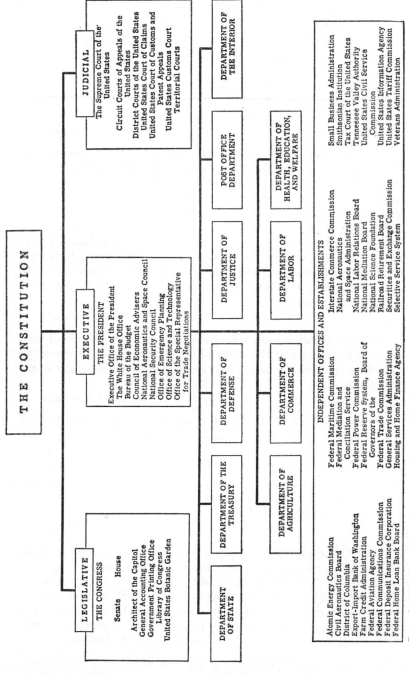

From the *U.S. Government Organization Manual* 1964–65.

SELF-SCORING EXAMINATION WITH ANSWERS

By Samuel Smith, Ph.D.

A Quick-Reference Aid to the Study of the U.S. Constitution and American Government

This self-scoring examination consists of three parts:

1. **VISUAL QUIZ** (on pages A, B, C, and D) with 28 questions. The answers (a, b, c, or d) must be written on the blank lines in the left and right margins of the page. After answering questions 1–28, the reader turns page B so that the correct printed answers appear next to his written answers. He can at once find his errors, analyze them, and study the explanations.

2. **COMPARISON TEST** (on pages E, F, G, and H) with 40 questions. The answers (T for True, or F for False) must be written on the blank lines in the left and right margins of the page. After answering questions 1–40, the reader turns page F so that the correct printed answers appear next to his written answers. He can at once find his errors, analyze them, and study the explanations.

3. **VISUAL SYNOPSIS** (on pages I, J, K, L, M, N, and O). Page I shows an over-all view of the federal governmental structure. This part includes 15 essay-type questions (on pages I, L, and M). The reader writes out answers in his own words and then compares his answers with the printed information on pages I–M. Additional important facts to review are given on pages N and O.

A

PART I. VISUAL QUIZ

For all questions 1–28, write your answers (a, b, c, or d) on the numbered lines in the margins. When you have answered all 28 questions, turn page B so that the printed answers on pages C and D will appear next to your answers. Study answers to questions you missed.

1._____

2._____

3._____

4._____

5._____

6._____

7._____

8._____

9._____

10._____

11._____

12._____

13._____

14._____

1. The Declaration of Independence expresses the
(a) divine rights theory of government
(b) government contract theory
(c) theory that the state arises from force
(d) evolutionary theory of origin of government

2. Voluntary associations replace the state under
(a) a totalitarian form of government
(b) individualism
(c) collectivism
(d) anarchism

3. By 1775 colonial assemblies had exclusive control over
(a) local government
(b) waging Indian wars
(c) taxes and appropriations
(d) colonial administration

4. In the colony of Virginia, the governor was
(a) appointed by the king
(b) elected annually
(c) selected by the Council
(d) chosen by the proprietor

5. Under Articles of Confederation
(a) each state had 1 vote
(b) the national courts were the supreme authority
(c) Congress imposed heavy taxes
(d) Congress elected the President

6. Authors of *The Federalist* were
(a) Samuel Adams and Patrick Henry
(b) Hamilton, Madison, and Jay
(c) Washington and Franklin
(d) Jefferson, Madison, and Jay

7. The Bill of Rights prohibited
(a) racial discrimination
(b) slavery
(c) excessive bail and cruel punishments
(d) suits against the states

8. The power of judicial review is
(a) enumerated
(b) reserved
(c) delegated
(d) implied

9. Eighteen specific powers of Congress are
(a) enumerated in the U.S. Constitution
(b) delegated to the states
(c) inherent
(d) implied

10. Constitutional amendments must be ratified by
(a) national referendum
(b) two-thirds of Congress
(c) legislatures or conventions in three-fourths of states
(d) two-thirds of state conventions called for this purpose

11. Recognition of foreign governments is a power of the
(a) Senate
(b) President
(c) State Department
(d) American ambassador

12. A bill of attainder refers to
(a) a retroactive law
(b) punishment of an individual without trial by legislative act
(c) an ex post facto law
(d) a *true bill*

13. Separation of powers is mainly a
(a) means for preventing dictatorship
(b) limitation on Congress
(c) restriction on the executive
(d) device to promote efficiency

14. In the vast majority of highly centralized governments,
(a) the national executive tends to be weak
(b) powers of local government tend to decline
(c) efficiency is impossible
(d) local initiative increases

PART I. VISUAL QUIZ (CONT.)

Questions 15–28

NOTE: Write your answers to questions 15–28 on the numbered lines at the right.

B

15. Due process refers mainly to
(a) police powers against crime
(b) moral behavior of individuals
(c) search of home without warrant
(d) limits on arbitrary government

16. A minority of voters can elect a President
(a) only if several candidates run
(b) only by means of proportional representation
(c) because of election-at-large
(d) because unit rule is illegal

17. All members of the President's Cabinet are
(a) approved by the House
(b) appointed (with Senate approval) by and responsible to President
(c) subject to impeachment in Supreme Court under Constitution
(d) subject to orders of Congress

18. The President can lawfully suspend or remove
(a) a member of Congress
(b) a quasi-judicial officer
(c) any judge too old to serve
(d) no judicial officer

19. The President can lawfully
(a) appropriate funds for defense
(b) revive an expired statute
(c) declare war without Congress
(d) involve the nation in war by ordering armed intervention abroad

20. If a treaty voids a federal law,
(a) the treaty is always superior
(b) the law takes precedence
(c) the most recent law or treaty is considered valid
(d) it cannot bind future Presidents

21. If a President waits 10 days, then returns unsigned bill to Congress,
(a) the bill is automatically killed
(b) a 2/3 vote for its passage is required
(c) the bill becomes law
(d) Congress must vote on the bill again and resubmit it

22. The Commission form of city government
(a) combines legislative and executive functions in one body
(b) divides authority between city manager and elected council
(c) is the Commission-Manager plan
(d) makes use of proportional representation

23. The House has great influence on foreign policy mainly because
(a) it must approve treaties
(b) it must approve war declaration
(c) it originates all revenue bills
(d) it has power to impeach the Secretary of State

24. The President can make rules with the force of law
(a) if Congress so empowers him
(b) without Senate approval
(c) only after Congress adjourns
(d) whenever Atty. Gen. approves

25. Congress' power to take a census and reapportion House seats is
(a) mandatory under Constitution
(b) usurped by Census Bureau
(c) concurrent with that of States
(d) subject to judicial control

26. Third parties are retarded by
(a) proportional representation
(b) the single-member representative district system
(c) use of the Australian ballot
(d) direct election of Senators

27. The U.S. Supreme Court can
(a) veto any act of Congress
(b) invalidate a bill when it is still in committee
(c) decide only specific cases
(d) render pre-trial decisions

28. In federal court civil cases,
(a) injunctions are not permissible
(b) felonies are often prosecuted
(c) the govt. may be a plaintiff
(d) the U.S. can usually be sued without its consent

(b)

(d)

(c)

(a)

(a)

(b)

(c)

(d)

(a)

(c)

(b)

(b)

(a)

(b)

1. The Declaration of Independence expresses the contract theory binding the king to rule justly. The king's violations of the contract released the people from their obligation to obey it and justified them in creating free and independent states.

2. Voluntary associations replace the state under anarchism, which considers the state an unnecessary restriction on liberty. Both collectivism and totalitarianism require centralized control.

3. By 1775 colonial assemblies had exclusive control over initiating tax laws and making appropriations. Governor was commander-in-chief, directed colonial and local administrations.

4. In the colony of Virginia, the governor was appointed by king as in all royal colonies; in charter colonies, elected annually; in proprietary, chosen by proprietor.

5. Under Articles of Confederation each state had 1 vote (& 2 to 7 congressmen), reflecting state sovereignty. There were no national courts, no taxing power, and no central executive.

6. Authors of *The Federalist* were Madison and Jay, working with Hamilton, not Jefferson. Adams opposed Constitution without a Bill of Rights. Washington decisively favored Constitution.

7. The Bill of Rights prohibited excessive bail, cruel punishments, government expropriation, conviction without fair trial, denial of free speech, etc., unreasonable searches. Ignored slavery.

8. The power of judicial review is implied because of (1)supremacy of Constitution and (2)duty of federal courts to disregard statute conflicting with Constitution.

9. Eighteen specific powers of Congress are enumerated in Art.I of Constitution. Implied powers are those necessary to execute specific enumerated powers. Inherent powers are those essential to sovereignty.

10.Constitutional amendments must be ratified by three-fourths of state legislatures or conventions. State can change its negative vote but not its acceptance once voted. Congress may set time limit; otherwise, proposal remains before the states.

11.Recognition of foreign governments is a power of the President, who acts by receiving envoys from abroad, appointing a diplomat, negotiating a treaty, or issuing a proclamation.

12.A bill of attainder refers to legislative condemnation without trial or other legal protection. A *true bill* is grand jury endorsement approving an indictment. (a) and (c) are identical.

13.Separation of powers is mainly a means of preventing dictatorship. The Constitution also contains checks and balances by which one division may partly control another.

14.In the vast majority of highly centralized governments, powers of local government tend to decline and to be taken over by the central government, especially by the executive. As U.S. national problems grew more complex, federal powers greatly expanded.

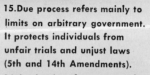

15. Due process refers mainly to limits on arbitrary government. It protects individuals from unfair trials and unjust laws (5th and 14th Amendments).

16. A minority of voters can elect a President because election-at-large method permits choice of many electors by narrow margins and nullifies huge majorities for electors in some other states.

17. All members of the President's Cabinet are responsible to President, who appoints (with Senate approval usually granted) and can remove them or suspend cabinet meetings; all civil officers are subject to removal by impeachment.

18. The President can lawfully suspend or remove no judicial or quasi-judicial or quasi-legislative officers. Judges can be impeached by House and tried by Senate.

19. The President can lawfully direct troops to intervene abroad and thus involve the nation in war, but only Congress can appropriate necessary funds. Senate could obstruct his appointments.

20. If a treaty voids a federal law, the courts will usually enforce the more recent expression of public will in law or treaty. Executive agreements, which are not submitted to Senate, fall under different rule.

21. If a President waits 10 days, then returns unsigned bill to Congress, the bill becomes law unless Congress has adjourned during the 10-day period, in which case the bill is void, as if it had been vetoed. This is the "pocket veto" whch cannot be overridden by houses of Congress.

22. The Commission form of city government concentrates legislative and executive powers in one elected body. Since each Commissioner heads a department, there is danger of administrative inefficiency, arbitrary decisions, and political interference.

23. The House has great influence on foreign policy mainly because it originates all money bills. Only the Senate votes on treaties. But both Houses must concur for war declaration. Secretary is responsible to President.

24. The President can make rules with the force of law when Congress grants him power to do so and sets forth objectives consistent with the U.S. Constitution.

25. Congress' power to take a census and reapportion House seats is mandatory. Article I requires reapportionment among states on basis of population. Census Bureau acts as agent of Congress.

26. Third parties are retarded by single-member district system nullifying minority vote in district. Proportional representation gives voice to minority, tending to create splinter parties.

27. The U.S. Supreme Court can decide specific cases brought by persons affected by a law. Only courts can decide what the law is and whether it conflicts with Constitution.

28. In federal court civil cases, the federal government may be a defendant or a plaintiff, but never a prosecutor; it cannot be sued without its consent. Injunctions are often granted.

(d)	15.____
(c)	16.____
(b)	17.____
(d)	18.____
(d)	19.____
(c)	20.____
(c)	21.____
(a)	22.____
(c)	23.____
(a)	24.____
(a)	25.____
(b)	26.____
(c)	27.____
(c)	28.____

(Study questions you missed. Then go on to Part II.)

E

PART II. COMPARISON TEST

For all questions 1—40, write your answers (T for True, or F for False) on the numbered lines in the margins. Then turn page F so that the printed answers on pages G and H appear next to your answers. Study answers to questions you missed.

1.——

2.——

3.——

4.——

5.——

6.——

7.——

8.——

9.——

10.——

11.——

12.——

13.——

14.——

15.——

16.——

17.——

18.——

19.——

20.——

1. **The 11th Amendment** prohibits the U.S.Supreme Court from taking action against the states.

2. **Delegates to the Constitutional Convention** were originally instructed to amend the Articles of Confederation, not to write a new Constitution.

3. **The legislative powers of state governments are** delegated to them by the national government and may be withdrawn by Congress.

4. **In 1789 all but a few believed that the vote should be granted** to all citizens, including the poorest nontaxpayers.

5. **The U.S.Constitution provides for freedom of speech** in time of peace, but not during war emergencies when military leaders control public opinion.

6. **The Populist Party of the 1890's advocated** a tax policy now part and parcel of the governing process.

7. **The U.S.Constitution provides that in national elections** all citizens 21 years or older will have the opportunity to vote.

8. **When the President vetoes a bill,** he may ignore it or return it unsigned to either House of Congress that he chooses.

9. **Urban areas in many states** are underrepresented in their legislature in proportion to their population.

10. **The U.S.Constitution** allows states to make interstate compacts which become effective when approved by Congress.

11. **American citizenship may be given up voluntarily** at any time, including a period of war emergency.

12. **The Pendleton Act of 1883 provided for** establishment of a Civil Service Commission and a Bureau of the Budget.

13. **Secretaries of the Army, Navy, and Air Force are subordinate** to the Joint Chiefs of Staff.

14. **The basis of U.S.citizenship is** application of two factors: the jus soli and the jus sanguinis.

15. **The U.N.Charter gives a veto power to** all 5 largest Powers for use in the Assembly and the Council.

16. **American municipalities are rightly considered creatures** of the federal government under the Constitution.

17. **A home rule charter for the typical American city** allows it perfect freedom to make its own laws without restriction.

18. **The U.S.Supreme Court may** declare part of a law unconstitutional without invalidating the entire law.

19. **The Supreme Court held that** Congress can create quasi-legislative bodies and prescribe the sole grounds for dismissal.

20. **Members of Congress cannot be arrested** during attendance at or on the way to Congress even on charges of committing a felony.

PART II. COMPARISON TEST (CONT.)
Questions 21–40
Write your answers (T or F) to these questions on the numbered lines at the right.

21. Congress can, if it chooses to do so,
    reorganize the executive branch of the federal government.

22. The size of the House of Representatives
    varies automatically with increases in population every ten years.

23. The Federal Government's principal source of revenue is
    the income made possible by the 16th Amendment.

24. To become a law a bill in Congress must be
    reported favorably by a standing committee of majority party.

25. The main purpose of efforts to reorganize state governments is
    to give less authority to the legislature and to decentralize.

26. If a majority on the Supreme Court cannot agree on a decision,
    the case must be settled outside of the federal courts.

27. Nominations in direct primary elections
    are regulated only by state laws, not by Congress.

28. Ability to read and write English
    is an unconstitutional requirement to keep some minorities from voting.

29. The Hatch Act limited the political campaign expenditures
    in national elections to 3 million dollars.

30. The functions and powers of a county govt. are usually
    granted by the state in a charter which lists each of the functions and powers.

31. In most states the Atty. General
    is nominated by the governor and approved by the state's legislature.

32. The 15th Amendment to the U.S. Constitution
    extended the franchise to all citizens, including illiterates and the insane.

33. In the case of McCulloch v. Maryland,
    the U.S. Supreme Court prevented a state from interfering with federal govt. activities.

34. In the case of Brown v. Bd. of Educ. of Topeka
    the Supreme Court reversed its "separate but equal" doctrine.

35. In 1959 an act passed by Congress
    admitted the territory of Hawaii into the U.S. as the 50th state of the Union.

36. In all suits at common law in state and federal courts,
    the 6th Amendment to the Constitution requires a jury trial.

37. A person violating both a state and a federal law in one act
    cannot be prosecuted by both state and federal officers.

38. The 8th Amendment provides that
    all accused persons must be released on reasonable bail.

39. The Civil Rights Act of 1957
    empowered new Division in Justice Dept. to get court injunctions to protect voting rights.

40. The U.S. Supreme Court has
    authority to judge qualifications of candidates for the House and Senate.

G

PART II. COMPARISON TEST (CONT.)

Answers to Questions 1—20

Compare your answers with the printed answers. Study answers to any questions you missed.

(F) **1. The 11th Amendment**
merely exempts states from suits
by citizens of other states or of
(T) foreign countries.

(F) **2. Delegates to the Constitutional Convention**
substituted a new constitution
(F) which became effective when
ratified by nine states.

(F) **3. The legislative powers of state governments are**
(T) reserved, not delegated, but must
give way to Constitutional federal
(F) powers in case of conflict.

(F) **4. In 1789 all but a few believed**
that the vote should be granted
only to the property owners and
(T) the taxpayers.

(T) **5. The U.S.Constitution provides for freedom of speech**
at all times. But it is limited
(F) by government's power of self-
preservation.

(F) **6. The Populist Party of the 1890's advocated**
(F) a graduated income tax made possible
by the 16th Amendment.

(T) **7. The U.S.Constitution provides that in national elections**
(F) states set voting qualifications
except as to color or sex.

(F) **8. When the President vetoes a bill,**
he returns it unsigned to the house
of origin with his objections within
(F) 10 days.

(T) **9. Urban areas in many states**
are underrepresented because
(T) historically dominant rural element
controls reapportionment.

(F) **10.The U.S.Constitution**
prohibits any state from making
agreements with other states without the consent of Congress.

11.American citizenship may be given up voluntarily
in wartime but only with the ap-
proval of the U.S.Atty. Gen.

12.The Pendleton Act of 1883 pro-vided for
a Civil Service Commission, but
the Bureau of the Budget was set
up in 1921.

13.Secretaries of the Army, Navy, and Air Force are subordinate
to the Secy. of Defense, who is a
civilian member of Cabinet.

14.The basis of U.S.citizenship is application of two factors:
birthplace; nationality of one's
parents.

15.The U.N.Charter gives a veto power to
5 major Powers for use only in
the Security Council.

16. American municipalities are rightly considered creatures
of state govt. which approves charters
and grants specific powers.

17.A home rule charter for the typical American city
grants much freedom, but subject to
state and federal laws.

18.The U.S.Supreme Court may
negate invalid parts of a law but
let valid parts stand if separable
from the other parts.

19.The Supreme Court held that
Congress can restrict the
President from dismissing
commissioners of quasi-
legislative or regulatory bodies.

20.Members of Congress cannot be arrested
for anything said in their speeches,
but they can be arrested at any time
for treason or a felony.

PART II. COMPARISON TEST (CONT.)
Answers to Questions 21–40

Compare your answers with the printed answers. Study answers to any questions you missed.

21. Congress can, if it chooses to do so,
create executive depts. and withhold funds from them. **(T) 21.____**

22. The size of the House of Representatives
is fixed by statute at 435 members (1941 amendment provides equal-proportions method of reapportionment). **(F) 22.____**

23. The Federal Government's principal source of revenue is
income tax: individual tax yields 50%; corporation tax 30%. **(T) 23.____**

24. To become a law a bill in Congress must be
passed by both Houses in identical form, submitted to President. **(F) 24.____**

25. The main purpose of efforts to reorganize state governments is
to increase powers of the governor over executive departments. **(F) 25.____**

26. If a majority on the Supreme Court cannot agree on a decision,
the decision of the next lower court will be enforced. **(F) 26.____**

27. Nominations in direct primary elections
are subject to state regulation (e.g., Conn. does not use primaries). **(T) 27.____**

28. Ability to read and write English
is constitutional requirement if uniformly applied by state. **(F) 28.____**

29. The Hatch Act limited the political campaign expenditures
amt. spent by natl. party but not amt. spent by state or local groups. **(T) 29.____**

30. The functions and powers of a county govt. are usually
delegated to the county govt. by the state in its statute laws or its constitution or both. **(F) 30.____**

31. In most states the Atty. General is elected by the voters and is often quite independent of the governor and the majority party. **(F) 31.____**

32. The 15th Amendment to the U.S. Constitution
merely guaranteed voting rights irrespective of race, color, or previous condition of servitude. **(F) 32.____**

33. In the case of McCulloch v. Maryland,
the Supreme Court prevented Md. from taxing and thus controlling a United States bank. **(T) 33.____**

34. In the case of Brown v. Bd. of Educ. of Topeka
the Court invalidated race discrimination in public schools. **(T) 34.____**

35. In 1959 an act passed by Congress
changed the status of Hawaii effective after a referendum of approval by the Hawaiian people. **(T) 35.____**

36. In all suits at common law in state and federal courts,
the 7th Amendment grants jury trial if more than $20 is involved. **(F) 36.____**

37. A person violating both a state and a federal law in one act
broke both laws, can be prosecuted by state and federal govts. **(F) 37.____**

38. The 8th Amendment provides that bail must be reasonable; it may be refused in capital crimes. **(F) 38.____**

39. The Civil Rights Act of 1957
permits contempt proceedings against persons violating court orders protecting voting rights. **(T) 39.____**

40. The U.S. Supreme Court has
no power to judge qualifications for Congress; each House judges qualifications of its own members. **(F) 40.____**

I

PART III. VISUAL SYNOPSIS
Write answers to questions I—V, below, and compare your answers with facts on
pages J and K. Then go on to questions VI and VII on page L.

THE U.S. CONSTITUTION

I. What are the 6 processes whereby the Constitution has been
greatly modified? Explain how each of these processes has
changed provisions or applications of the Constitution. (See Page J)

II. What are 6 basic principles underlying the U.S. Constitution? (See Page J)

LEGISLATURE	EXECUTIVE	JUDICIARY
III. Name 6 types of non-legislative and 8 types of legislative powers of Congress.	IV. What 11 kinds of activities are within the scope of the President's authority?	V. State the main classes of legal cases decided by the federal courts.
(See Page K)	(See Page K)	

10 DEPTS. (In Order of Possible Succession to Presidency)

1. State Dept.: conducts foreign affairs; controls overseas representatives; negotiates treaties; work in international agencies; information services; passports; acts as home office.

2. Treasury: collects customs, duties, and taxes; prints money; supervises federal expenditures; manages public debt; directs Secret Service, Narcotics Squad, national banks.

3. Defense: runs Army, Navy, Air Force, and advisory agencies (top advisors are Army, Navy, and Air Force Secretaries and Chairman of Joint Chiefs of Staff).

4. Justice: Attorney General, legal adviser of Pres., conducts U.S. cases; FBI, federal prisons; immigration and naturalization; executes federal court orders.

5. Post Office: mail; COD's; postal savings; stamps; P.O. inspectors cooperate with Justice Department.

6. Interior: fish and wildlife; mineral resources; public lands management; water and power development; Indian affairs; national parks; Geological Survey; reclamation; Bureau of Mines.

7. Agriculture: research on soils, forestry, etc.; training and advisory programs; marketing (data and regulation); aid to farmers (credit and insurance; rural electrification).

8. Commerce: foreign trade; Patent Office; Census Bureau; Civil Aeronautics Admin.; public roads; Bureau of Standards; Business Economics; Geodetic Survey.

9. Labor: statistics; employment services; administers labor laws.

10. Health, Education, and Welfare: research; social security programs; Food and Drug Admin.; aid for handicapped persons. (Not in line of succession to Presidency.)

INDEPENDENT AGENCIES, responsible to Congress and the President, combine legislative and judicial functions. Their technical experts facilitate execution of Congressional policies. Independent agencies are of several types:

(1) regulating agencies, which combine legislative and judicial functions and operate in accord with Administrative Procedure Act of Congress. Examples: Civil Service Comm.; Fed. Communications Comm.; Fed. Trade Comm.; Interstate Commerce Comm.; Natl. Labor Relations Board (NLRB); Securities Exchange Comm.; U.S. Tariff Comm.

(2) agencies outside departmental system: e.g., Agency for Internatl. Development; Central Intelligence Agency; Export-Import Bank; Fed. Reserve System; Natl. Aeronautics and Space Admin. (NASA); Natl. Mediation Bd.; Selective Service System; Veterans Administration.

(3) govt. corporations: e.g., Fed. Deposit Insurance Corp.; Tenn. Valley Authority (TVA).

THE U.S. CONSTITUTION
ratified by 9 states, June 1788 (excluding NY and Va.)

sets forth 6 fundamental principles: (1)Popular sovereignty with limited government. (2)Federalism, with power shared by states and central government. (3)Powers not enumerated must be reserved for the states or people. (4)Supremacy of national government protected from state taxation or interference—U.S. courts to decide conflicts. (5) Separation of powers among executive, legislative, and judicial branches. (6)Supremacy of the judiciary in deciding Constitutional issues.

The Constitution has changed through 6 processes:(1)amendment;(2)passage of laws by Congress;(3)judicial interpretation;(4)influence of political parties;(5)influence of President;(6)changing customs. (See discussion of the 6 processes, below.)

The Constitution has 7 Articles and 22 Amendments(1-10,Bill of Rights)

Articles:

I. Legislative dept.:organization, powers, restraints

II. Executive dept.:powers, restraints, duties, election of President

III. Judicial dept.:powers, restraints, treason defined

IV. Powers of states. Relation of states and territories to federal government

V. Method of amending Constitution

VI. National debts; supremacy of Constitution, federal laws and treaties; pledge of officials; no religious test for public office

VII. Method for ratification

Amendments:

1-10:Bill of Rights. 11:Exemption of states from suit. 12:New method of electing President. 13:Slavery prohibited. 14:Protection of citizen's rights(due process). 15:Right to vote. 16:Income tax. 17:Popular election of senators. 18:Prohibition. 19:Woman suffrage. 20:Abolition of lame duck session. 21: Repeal of 18th. 22:Limitation of President to 2 elective terms. 23: Wash., D.C., voting rights.

Passage of Laws by Congress:
Congress interprets broadly its duties stated or implied by the Constitution. E.g., it established the Civil Service System (1883) under Art.II Sec.2 which gives Congress authority to vest the appointment of "such inferior officers . . . in the President alone, in the courts of law, or in the heads of depts." Laws regulating mfg., farming, and public utilities, laws on national defense and foreign affairs, and laws providing education are other examples of broad interpretation.

Judicial Interpretation:
The courts have changed the interpretations to meet changing conditions. Thus, minimum wage laws and federal taxes on state employees were once invalid. Marbury v. Madison(1803)set precedent for court supremacy in interpretation.

Influence of Political Parties:
Political parties have modified the Constitution through method of electing President and pressure on Congress and President. Even minor parties have influenced interpretation by popularizing social reforms later espoused by the two major parties.

Influence of President:
The President has often applied his own interpretations of the Constitution, as in claiming right to send troops abroad to protect American property.

Changing Customs:
Changing customs have modified the Constitution, as in development of the President's Cabinet or legislative committees, or "senatorial courtesy" (whereby senator blocks appointment of objectionable nominee from his home state).

K

VISUAL SYNOPSIS   (CONT.)

NOTE: The information below answers questions III–V and also includes basic additional facts about the three branches of the federal government.

LEGISLATURE	EXECUTIVE	JUDICIARY
Non-legislative powers: constituent; electoral; judicial; executive; administrative; and investigative. Its legislative powers are: enumerated; implied; resultant; emergency; mandatory; permissive; exclusive; and concurrent.	Powers cover: law enforcement; military; appointment and removal; foreign affairs; pardon and reprieve; messages to Congress; veto; special sessions of Congress; budget; executive ordinances; contacts with political leaders.	Decides cases involving: the Constitution; federal laws; treaties; admiralty and maritime affairs; foreign representatives or nations; U.S. as a party; different states or citizens of different states.
Two senators from each of 50 states; house membership for each based on population as determined by Census Bureau. State designation of Congressional districts permits gerrymandering. Representative must be 25 yrs. or older, resident of his state, and U.S. citizen 7 yrs. or more. Each house judges election results and qualifications of its members. House term, 2 yrs.; Senate, 6 yrs. Senator must be 30 yrs. or older, resident of his state, U.S. citizen 9 yrs. or more; 17th Amendment provided for direct election by people instead of by state legislatures. In House, Speaker is majority leader; in Senate, U.S. Vice-Pres. presides. A bill is referred to 1 of 19 standing committees in House, to 1 of 15 in Senate; these are decisive for legislation.	**White House Office** has an Asst. to the Pres. and several secretaries, 4 administrative. **Bureau of the Budget** prepares and supervises budget; advises on work of all govt. agencies and on proposed legislation. **Council of Economic Advisors** advises Pres. on economic problems and policies, helps him prepare economic reports. **National Security Council** assists Pres. to execute programs, domestic and foreign, to safeguard national security. **Office of Emergency Planning** aids in mobilization of national resources for defense. **Office of Science and Tech.** **QUALIFICATIONS:** Pres. and Vice-Pres.—35 yrs. or older, U.S. resident 14 yrs. or more, native-born citizen. **REMOVAL:** only by impeachment.	U.S. Supreme Court (Chief Justice, 8 Assoc. Justices) judges original cases (1) affecting ambassadors, etc. and (2) involving a state; it judges all other cases of law and constitutionality which come to it on appeal or writ from state courts or are referred to it from lower federal courts. The 90 district courts (about 300 judges) render decisions which can be appealed to Circuit Courts (11 in 11 circuits). Circuit Court decisions are usually final unless Supreme Court intervenes, to decide a major constitutional or legal point. Special courts: U.S. Court of Claims (suits vs. U.S.); U.S. Court of Customs and Patent Appeals; U.S. Customs Court; Territorial Courts; Court of Military Appeals; Tax Court. Federal judges are nominated by Pres., confirmed by Senate. They can be removed only by impeachment.

L

VISUAL SYNOPSIS   (CONT.)

NOTE: For essay-type questions VI—XV (pages L and M) write your answers out and compare them with the information on pages L, M, and N.

VI. Discuss ten important constitutional cases. (Compare your answers with the list below.)

CONSTITUTIONAL CASES

1. **Marbury v. Madison** (1803) voided act of Congress giving court greater jurisdiction than that fixed in Art. III.
2. **Dartmouth Coll. v. Woodward** (1819): corporate charters cannot be nullified by a state.
3. **McCulloch v. Md.** (1819): state cannot tax (and thus possibly destroy) a U.S. instrumentality.
4. **Dred Scott v. Sanford** (1857): slave not a citizen with right to sue in U.S. courts.
5. **Wabash, St. Louis, and Pacific v. Ill.** (1886): state cannot regulate that portion of interstate journey in state.
6. **Lochner v. N.Y.** (1905): state fixing of maximum hrs. violates freedom of contract (14th Amend.). Reversed in Bunting v. Oregon, 1917).
7. **Adkins v. Children's Hospital** (1923): federal regulation of minimum wages unconstitutional (reversed in West Coast Hotel v. Parrish, 1937).
8. **N.L.R.B. v. Jones & Laughlin** (1937): industries organized on natl. scale are subject to interstate commerce power of Congress.
9. **U.S. v. Darby** (1941): upheld Fair Labor Standards Act setting maximum hrs. and minimum wages and also prohibiting interstate shipment of goods produced by child labor.
10. **Brown v. Bd. of Educ. of Topeka** (1954): race segregation in public schools unconstitutional (reversing "separate but equal" doctrine of Plessy v. Ferguson, 1896).

VII. Discuss the basic constitutional rights of citizens and states. (Compare your answer with the list below.)

CONSTITUTIONAL RIGHTS

1. Writ of habeas corpus requires prompt justice for any prisoner. Art. I, Sec. 9.
2. Bills of attainder and ex post facto laws prohibited. Art I, Secs. 9, 10.
3. Jury trial in criminal cases, Art. III, Sec. 3; in civil cases, 7th Amendment.
4. Treason narrowly defined to protect innocent and heirs of guilty. Art. III.
5. Laws vs. freedoms of speech, religion, press, or assembly forbidden. 1st Amendment.
6. Peacetime right to refuse quartering of soldiers in one's home. 3rd Amendment.
7. Protection vs. unreasonable searches and seizures. 4th Amendment.
8. Double jeopardy forbidden; no criminal prosecution unless grand jury indicts; no one compelled to testify against self· due process of law to protect life, liberty, property. 5th Amendment.
9. Prompt, public trial of accused person in state and district of the crime; charges and witnesses to be presented; right to legal counsel. 6th Amendment.
10. Jury trial in civil cases involving $20 or more in value. 7th Amendment.
11. Excessive bail or fines and cruel punishments prohibited. 8th Amendment.
12. Freedom to vote irrespective of race, color, sex; qualifications must apply to all. 15th and 19th Amendments.
13. State laws must not impair obligations of a contract. Art. I, Sec. 10.
14. Each state must give citizens of other states the same privileges and immunities as those accorded to its own citizens. 14th Amendment.
15. Each state must give full faith and credit to acts of other states. Art. IV.

M

COLONIAL GOVERNMENTS

VIII. What documents and practices of the mother country formed the basis for American traditions of self-government?

IX. Who had final authority in the colonies in 1775?

COLONIAL GOVERNMENTS

Traditions of self-govt. were based on the British Magna Charta, Petition of Right, Bill of Rights (1689), common law, independent judiciary, bicameral legislature. In 1775 royal colonies were governed by officers of the King; laws in proprietary colonies (except Md.) were subject to Royal approval; not so in charter colonies.

ARTICLES OF CONFEDERATION

X. What were 5 principal features of the Articles of Confederation?

XI. State reasons for the failure of the Confederation.

ARTICLES OF CONFEDERATION, 1781

Features state sovereignty; unicameral govt. by delegates of state legislatures; no central executive or judiciary; authority— no power over taxes, commerce, tariff barriers, individuals; amendments required unanimity. Failure due to: financial troubles, currency depreciation, commercial warfare, lack of state cooperation.

CONSTITUTIONAL CONVENTION

XII. Who were the delegates to the Constitutional Convention?

XIII. Describe the Virginia Plan.

CONSTITUTIONAL CONVENTION, 1787

11 states sent delegates, mainly leading lawyers, businessmen, politicians. Each state had 1 vote; majority ruled.

Virginia Plan proposed lower house elected by people, upper house by lower house from list submitted by state legislatures. State's voting power in Congress to depend on taxes paid, population or both. Congress could veto state laws. Congress to choose national executive and national judges.

Pinckney Plan proposed Pres. with 7-yr. term chosen by Congress (bicameral as above); each legislator to have 1 vote.

New Jersey Plan: 1-house Congress to elect Pres. who elects judges. Each state to have equal representation in Congress.

Conn. Compromise: House based on population; Senate representation equal for all states.

Three-fifths Compromise: three-fifths of slaves counted for direct taxes and for representation in Congress.

EARLY STATE GOVERNMENTS

XIV. What were the democratic principles of the early state governments of 1775-1781?

XV. In what respect were they undemocratic?

EARLY STATE GOVERNMENTS, 1775-1781

The Revolutionary state govts. observed principles of popular sovereignty, limited govt., individual rights, separation of powers, and legislative supremacy. But all the states sharply limited suffrage. Governors had little power; most of them were elected (by the people or the legislatures) for 1-yr. terms.

Usually the lower house, elected by the voters for 1-yr. term, favored the rank and file. The upper house, elected by the voters or by the lower house for 1 to 5 yr. terms, often favored property owners. In most states, judges were appointed by governor or legislature (popularly elected in Ga.) and could be removed by legislature.

Conn. and R.I. retained their charters.

Mass. did not adopt her constitution until 1780.

TYPES OF GOVERNMENT

Anarchist: opposes all govt. controls. **Individualist:** favor govt. action to preserve order and protect personal rights. **Totalitarianism:** advocates govt. control over all important matters (Communists oppose private ownership; fascist totalitarians accept it). **Collectivist:** demands more govt. control in matters affecting public welfare, with less reliance on individual's self-direction.

Major Types: autocracy (1-man rule); oligarchy (rule by few); democracy (rule by people directly or, in a republic, by their representatives mainly); unitary (1 central authority provided); federal (power shared with states).

The U.S. is a federal, democratic republic (people in 50 states elect representatives) with a written constitution and Presidential govt. Great Britain is a unitary democracy with an unwritten constitution and a parliamentary govt. (the executive is responsible to the legislature). Soviet Russia is a totalitarian dictatorship which claims to be progressing toward a collective, Communist state; it differs from Socialism elsewhere, which advocates a more peaceful, gradual increase in collective authority without dictatorship. Laissez-faire is the theory directly opposed to increased govt. control of individuals.

MODERN STATE GOVERNMENTS

State Constitutions: contain bill of rights; provide for legislative, executive, and judicial depts.; define relations between state and local govts.; fix qualifications for suffrage; and often regulate important matters, such as taxation, finance, public utilities, etc. Constitutional conventions (except in R.I.) can propose revisions for popular referendum. Some state legislatures have appointed commissions to prepare the proposals.

State Legislatures: range in size from 43 members in 1-house system of Neb. to 424 in 2-chamber system of N.H. Terms are 2 or 4 yrs. (senators serve 2 yrs. in 15 states, 4 yrs. in 35 states; representatives serve 2 yrs. in 45 states). Constitutions in 36 states give legislatures control over apportionment of seats. Legislatures enact laws on education, elections, finance, highways, insurance, labor, libraries, mental health, taxes, water resources, status and work of women, etc.

State Judiciary: highest court; superior; county or district or circuit courts; and special courts (surrogate, municipal, justices of the peace, juvenile, magistrates', small claims, etc.). Often the judges are elected (in a few states appointed by legislature or governor).

Executive: in 34 states governor serves 4 yrs., in 16 he serves 2 yrs. Highest officers (Secy. of State, Treasurer, Auditor, Atty. Gen.) usually elected; in many states lesser officers appointed by governor.

THEORIES OF ORIGINS OF GOVERNMENT

Elements necessary for any govt. are: people; territory; unity; political institutions; sovereign power; and continuity.

Competing Theories:

Divine Rights, with the king as the inheritor of authority from a divine source—the historical basis of monarchy.

Govt. Contract theory (adopted in the Declaration of Independence) that govt. is based on an agreement between the people and their rulers.

Force Theory (of govt. through right of conquest) is always inadequate explanation.

Anthropological (or **Evolutionary**) theory states that govt. developed when customs became fixed and had to be enforced by some authority—the favored theory.

MODERN LOCAL GOVERNMENT

County Govts. (ranging from 3 in Del. to 254 in Texas): officers derive powers from state govts.; administer state laws; collect local taxes, prosecute criminals; supervise elections, educational institutions, health and welfare programs, highway construction and maintenance, etc. Bd. of Supervisors and other county officials, such as sheriff, clerk, superintendent of schools, coroner, assessor, treasurer, and recorder of deeds are usually elected.

Towns: in New England are the principal units of local government; elsewhere towns or townships are subordinate to counties.

Municipal Govts.: operate under charter system as corporations with proprietary and governmental powers. Charters may be: special—granted by legislature; general—identical for all cities in state; classified—based on population groupings; optional—with cities choosing their form through a referendum; home-rule—in about 200 cities in 24 states.

Types of City Govt.: Mayor-council (elected mayor and city council); commission plan (5 members replace mayor and council), combining legislative with executive powers; council-manager plan (manager selected by city council to direct city affairs); and proportional-representation-city manager plan (with commissioners elected by proportional representation).

PASSAGE OF LAW

Each committee of Congress reports on original or amended bill which (if cleared by majority leader in Senate or Rules Committee in House) is debated, amended, and approved before being sent to the other house where their committee reports. The bill is debated, etc., in 2nd house. Conferees meet to iron out differences; the bill is then sent to the President.

SUCCESSION TO PRESIDENCY

By law of 1947: Speaker of House follows Vice-Pres.; then Pres. pro tem of Senate, Secs. of State, Treasury, Defense, Atty. Gen., Postmaster Gen., Secs. of Interior, Agriculture, Commerce, and Labor.

U.S. SUPREME COURT

Concurring and dissenting opinions are usually written; if majority cannot agree, lower court decision stands.

At the age of 70, following 20 yrs. of service, justices can retire at full pay.

FIELDS OF STUDY

Besides political theory, major fields of study include: constitutions and constitutional law (written or unwritten, with interpretations by courts, legislatures, or executives); international relations and organizations, including international law and diplomacy; comparative govt.; political processes, such as parties, elections, propaganda, law-making; and public administration (especially fiscal, personnel, and judicial problems involved in the management of public affairs).

INDEX GUIDE TO THE CONSTITUTION

PREAMBLE

ARTICLE I

Legislative Department: organization, powers, and restraints.

ARTICLE II

Executive Department: powers, restraints, duties and election of the President.

ARTICLE III

Judicial Department: powers, restraints. Definition of treason.

ARTICLE IV

Relation of States to each other and to the Federal Government. Guarantees to States. Government of Territories.

ARTICLE V

Method of Amending Constitution. Guarantee of equal representation of States in the United States Senate.

ARTICLE VI

Provision for national debts. Supremacy of the United States Constitution, Federal laws and treaties. Pledge of national and state officials to uphold Constitution. No religious test required as qualification to public office.

ARTICLE VII

Method for ratification of the Constitution.

AMENDMENTS

The first ten Amendments are frequently referred to as the *Bill of Rights*.

I   Freedom of Religion, Speech, the Press. Right to petition.

II   Right to keep and bear arms.

III   Quartering of soldiers.

IV   Limitation on searches and seizures.

V   Protection of accused in capital crimes.

VI   Right to speedy trial for accused.

VII   Trial by Jury in law-suits.

VIII   Excessive bail or unusual punishment forbidden.

IX   Peoples' rights retained.

X   Undelegated powers revert to the States or to the people.

XI   Exemption of states from suit by citizens of other states.

XII   New method of electing President (Supersedes part of Article II, Sec. 1).

XIII   Slavery prohibited.

XIV   Protection of citizens' rights.
Apportionment of Representatives in Congress (Supersedes Part of Article I, Sec. 2).
Status of officials engaged in insurrection.
Validity of war debt.

XV   Right of citizens to vote.

XVI   Income Tax.

XVII   Election of Senators.
Senatorial vacancies.

XVIII   Prohibition of intoxicating liquors.

XIX   Woman Suffrage.

XX   Abolition of "Lame Duck" session of Congress. Change in the date of assembly.

XXI   Repeal of Eighteenth Amendment.

XXII   Limitation of President's elective terms in office.

XXIII   Presidential vote for District of Columbia.

XXIV   Poll tax prohibited in national elections.

CONSTITUTION OF THE UNITED STATES

Adopted September 17, 1787
Effective March 4, 1789

WE the people of the United States, in order to form a more perfect union, establish justice, insure domestic tranquillity, provide for the common defense, promote the general welfare, and secure the blessings of liberty to ourselves and our posterity, do ordain and establish this Constitution for the United States of America.

ARTICLE I

SECTION 1. All legislative powers herein granted shall be vested in a Congress of the United States, which shall consist of a Senate and House of Representatives.

SECTION 2. 1. The House of Representatives shall be composed of members chosen every second year by the people of the several States, and the electors in each State shall have the qualifications requisite for electors of the most numerous branch of the State legislature.

2. No person shall be a representative who shall not have attained to the age of twenty-five years, and been seven years a citizen of the United States, and who shall not, when elected, be an inhabitant of that State in which he shall be chosen.

3. Representatives and direct taxes[1] shall be apportioned among the several States which may be included within this Union, according to their respective numbers, which shall be determined by adding to the whole number of free persons, including those bound to service for a term of years, and excluding Indians not taxed, *three fifths of all other persons.*[2] The actual enumeration shall be made within three years after the first meeting of the Congress of the United States, and within every subsequent term of ten years, in such manner as they shall by law direct. The number of representatives shall not exceed one for every thirty thousand, but each State shall have at least one representative; and until such enumeration shall be made, the State of New

---

[1] See the 16th Amendment.
[2] See the 14th Amendment.

Hampshire shall be entitled to choose three, Massachusetts eight, Rhode Island and Providence Plantations one, Connecticut five, New York six, New Jersey four, Pennsylvania eight, Delaware one, Maryland six, Virginia ten, North Carolina five, South Carolina five, and Georgia three.

4. When vacancies happen in the representation from any State, the executive authority thereof shall issue writs of election to fill such vacancies.

5. The House of Representatives shall choose their speaker and other officers; and shall have the sole power of impeachment.

SECTION 3. 1. The Senate of the United States shall be composed of two senators from each State, *chosen by the legislature thereof*,[1] for six years; and each senator shall have one vote.

2. Immediately after they shall be assembled in consequence of the first election, they shall be divided as equally as may be into three classes. The seats of the senators of the first class shall be vacated at the expiration of the second year, of the second class at the expiration of the fourth year, and of the third class at the expiration of the sixth year, so that one third may be chosen every second year; and if vacancies happen by resignation, or otherwise, during the recess of the legislature of any State, the executive thereof may make temporary appointments until the next meeting of the legislature, which shall then fill such vacancies.[1]

3. No person shall be a senator who shall not have attained to the age of thirty years, and been nine years a citizen of the United States, and who shall not, when elected, be an inhabitant of that State for which he shall be chosen.

4. The Vice President of the United States shall be President of the Senate, but shall have no vote, unless they be equally divided.

5. The Senate shall choose their other officers, and also a president *pro tempore,* in the absence of the Vice President, or when he shall exercise the office of the President of the United States.

6. The Senate shall have the sole power to try all impeachments. When sitting for that purpose, they shall be on oath or affirmation. When the President of the United States is tried, the chief justice

---

[1] See the 17th Amendment.

shall preside: and no person shall be convicted without the concurrence of two thirds of the members present.

7. Judgment in cases of impeachment shall not extend further than to removal from office, and disqualifications to hold and enjoy any office of honor, trust or profit under the United States: but the party convicted shall nevertheless be liable and subject to indictment, trial, judgment and punishment, according to law.

SECTION 4. 1. The times, places, and manner of holding elections for senators and representatives, shall be prescribed in each State by the legislature thereof; but the Congress may at any time by law make or alter such regulations, except as to the places of choosing senators.

2. The Congress shall assemble at least once in every year, and such meeting shall be on the first Monday in December, unless they shall by law appoint a different day.

SECTION 5. 1. Each House shall be the judge of the elections, returns and qualifications of its own members, and a majority of each shall constitute a quorum to do business; but a smaller number may adjourn from day to day, and may be authorized to compel the attendance of absent members, in such manner, and under such penalties as each House may provide.

2. Each House may determine the rules of its proceedings, punish its members for disorderly behavior, and, with the concurrence of two thirds, expel a member.

3. Each House shall keep a journal of its proceedings, and from time to time publish the same, excepting such parts as may in their judgment require secrecy; and the yeas and nays of the members of either House on any question shall, at the desire of one fifth of those present, be entered on the journal.

4. Neither House, during the session of Congress, shall, without the consent of the other, adjourn for more than three days, nor to any other place than that in which the two Houses shall be sitting.

SECTION 6. 1. The senators and representatives shall receive a compensation for their services, to be ascertained by law, and paid out of the Treasury of the United States. They shall in all cases, except treason, felony, and breach of the peace, be privileged from arrest during their attendance at the session of their respective Houses, and in going to and returning from the same; and for any speech or debate in either House, they shall not be questioned in any other place.

2. No senator or representative shall, during the time for which he was elected, be appointed to any civil office under the authority of the United States, which shall have been created, or the emoluments whereof shall have been increased during such time; and no person holding any office under the United States shall be a member of either House during his continuance in office.

Section 7. 1. All bills for raising revenue shall originate in the House of Representatives; but the Senate may propose or concur with amendments as on other bills.

2. Every bill which shall have passed the House of Representatives and the Senate, shall, before it becomes a law, be presented to the President of the United States; if he approves he shall sign it, but if not he shall return it, with his objections to that House in which it shall have originated, who shall enter the objections at large on their journal, and proceed to reconsider it. If after such reconsideration two thirds of that House shall agree to pass the bill, it shall be sent, together with the objections, to the other House, by which it shall likewise be reconsidered, and if approved by two thirds of that House, it shall become a law. But in all such cases the votes of both Houses shall be determined by yeas and nays, and the names of the persons voting for and against the bill shall be entered on the journal of each House respectively. If any bill shall not be returned by the President within ten days (Sundays excepted) after it shall have been presented to him, the same shall be a law, in like manner as if he had signed it, unless the Congress by their adjournment prevent its return, in which case it shall not be a law.

3. Every order, resolution, or vote to which the concurrence of the Senate and the House of Representatives may be necessary (except on a question of adjournment) shall be presented to the President of the United States; and before the same shall take effect, shall be approved by him, or being disapproved by him, shall be repassed by two thirds of the Senate and House of Representatives, according to the rules and limitations prescribed in the case of a bill.

Section 8. The Congress shall have the power

1. To lay and collect taxes, duties, imposts, and excises, to pay

the debts and provide for the common defense and general welfare of the United States; but all duties, imposts, and excises shall be uniform throughout the United States;

2. To borrow money on the credit of the United States;

3. To regulate commerce with foreign nations, and among the several States, and with the Indian tribes;

4. To establish a uniform rule of naturalization, and uniform laws on the subject of bankruptcies throughout the United States;

5. To coin money, regulate the value thereof, and of foreign coin, and fix the standard of weights and measures;

6. To provide for the punishment of counterfeiting the securities and current coin of the United States;

7. To establish post offices and post roads;

8. To promote the progress of science and useful arts, by securing for limited times to authors and inventors the exclusive right to their respective writings and discoveries;

9. To constitute tribunals inferior to the Supreme Court;

10. To define and punish piracies and felonies committed on the high seas, and offenses against the law of nations;

11. To declare war, grant letters of marque and reprisal, and make rules concerning captures on land and water;

12. To raise and support armies, but no appropriation of money to that use shall be for a longer term than two years;

13. To provide and maintain a navy;

14. To make rules for the government and regulation of the land and naval forces;

15. To provide for calling forth the militia to execute the laws of the Union, suppress insurrections and repel invasions;

16. To provide for organizing, arming, and disciplining the militia, and for governing such part of them as may be employed in the service of the United States, reserving to the States respectively, the appointment of the officers, and the authority of training the militia according to the discipline prescribed by Congress;

17. To exercise exclusive legislation in all cases whatsoever, over

such district (not exceeding ten miles square) as may, by cession of particular States, and the acceptance of Congress, become the seat of the government of the United States, and to exercise like authority over all places purchased by the consent of the legislature of the State in which the same shall be, for the erection of forts, magazines, arsenals, dockyards, and other needful buildings; and

18. To make all laws which shall be necessary and proper for carrying into execution the foregoing powers, and all other powers vested by this Constitution in the government of the United States, or in any department or officer thereof.

SECTION 9. 1. The migration or importation of such persons as any of the States now existing shall think proper to admit, shall not be prohibited by the Congress prior to the year one thousand eight hundred and eight, but a tax or duty may be imposed on such importation, not exceeding ten dollars for each person.

2. The privilege of the writ of *habeas corpus* shall not be suspended, unless when in cases of rebellion or invasion the public safety may require it.

3. No bill of attainder or *ex post facto* law shall be passed.

4. No capitation, or other direct, tax shall be laid, unless in proportion to the census or enumeration hereinbefore directed to be taken.[1]

5. No tax or duty shall be laid on articles exported from any State.

6. No preference shall be given by any regulation of commerce or revenue to the ports of one State over those of another: nor shall vessels bound to, or from, one State be obliged to enter, clear, or pay duties in another.

7. No money shall be drawn from the treasury, but in consequence of appropriations made by law; and a regular statement and account of the receipts and expenditures of all public money shall be published from time to time.

8. No title of nobility shall be granted by the United States: and no person holding any office of profit or trust under them, shall,

---

[1] See the 16th Amendment.

without the consent of the Congress, accept of any present, emolument, office, or title, of any kind whatever, from any king, prince, or
foreign State.

SECTION 10.   1.   No State shall enter into any treaty, alliance, or
confederation; grant letters of marque and reprisal; coin money; emit
bills of credit; make anything but gold and silver coin a tender in
payment of debts; pass any bill of attainder, *ex post facto* law, or law
impairing the obligation of contracts, or grant any title of nobility.

2.   No State shall, without the consent of the Congress, lay any
imposts or duties on imports or exports, except what may be absolutely
necessary for executing its inspection laws; and the net produce of
all duties and imposts laid by any State on imports or exports, shall
be for the use of the treasury of the United States; and all such laws
shall be subject to the revision and control of the Congress.

3.   No State shall, without the consent of the Congress, lay any
duty of tonnage, keep troops, or ships of war in time of peace, enter
into any agreement or compact with another State, or with a foreign
power, or engage in war, unless actually invaded, or in such imminent
danger as will not admit of delay.

ARTICLE II

SECTION 1.   1.   The executive power shall be vested in a President
of the United States of America. He shall hold his office during the
term of four years, and, together with the Vice President, chosen for
the same term, be elected as follows:

2.   Each State shall appoint, in such manner as the legislature
thereof may direct, a number of electors, equal to the whole number
of senators and representatives to which the State may be entitled
in the Congress: but no senator or representative, or person holding
an office of trust or profit under the United States, shall be appointed
an elector.

The electors shall meet in their respective States, and vote by ballot
for two persons, of whom one at least shall not be an inhabitant of the
same State with themselves. And they shall make a list of all the
persons voted for, and of the number of votes for each; which list
they shall sign and certify, and transmit sealed to the seat of the government of the United States, directed to the president of the Senate.
The president of the Senate shall, in the presence of the Senate and

House of Representatives, open all the certificates, and the votes shall then be counted. The person having the greatest number of votes shall be the President, if such number be a majority of the whole number of electors appointed; and if there be more than one who have such majority, and have an equal number of votes, then the House of Representatives shall immediately choose by ballot one of them for President; and if no person have a majority, then from the five highest on the list the said House shall in like manner choose the President. But in choosing the President, the votes shall be taken by States, the representation from each State having one vote; a quorum for this purpose shall consist of a member or members from two thirds of the States, and a majority of all the States shall be necessary to a choice. In every case, after the choice of the President, the person having the greatest number of votes of the electors shall be the Vice President. But if there should remain two or more who have equal votes, the Senate shall choose from them by ballot the Vice President.[1]

3. The Congress may determine the time of choosing the electors, and the day on which they shall give their votes; which day shall be the same throughout the United States.

4. No person except a natural born citizen, or a citizen of the United States, at the time of the adoption of this Constitution, shall be eligible to the office of President; neither shall any person be eligible to that office who shall not have attained to the age of thirty-five years, and been fourteen years a resident within the United States.

5. In case of the removal of the President from office, or of his death, resignation, or inability to discharge the powers and duties of the said office, the same shall devolve on the Vice President, and the Congress may by law provide for the case of removal, death, resignation, or inability, both of the President and Vice President, declaring what officer shall then act as President, and such officer shall act accordingly, until the disability be removed, or a President shall be elected.

6. The President shall, at stated times, receive for his services a compensation, which shall neither be increased nor diminished during the period for which he shall have been elected, and he shall not receive within that period any other emolument from the United States, or any of them.

---

[1] Superseded by the 12th Amendment.

7. Before he enter on the execution of his office, he shall take the following oath or affirmation: — "I do solemnly swear (or affirm) that I will faithfully execute the office of President of the United States, and will to the best of my ability, preserve, protect and defend the Constitution of the United States."

SECTION 2. 1. The President shall be commander in chief of the army and navy of the United States, and of the militia of the several States, when called into the actual service of the United States; he may require the opinion, in writing, of the principal officer in each of the executive departments, upon any subject relating to the duties of their respective offices, and he shall have power to grant reprieves and pardons for offenses against the United States, except in cases of impeachment.

2. He shall have power, by and with the advice and consent of the Senate, to make treaties, provided two thirds of the senators present concur; and he shall nominate, and by and with the advice and consent of the Senate, shall appoint ambassadors, other public ministers and consuls, judges of the Supreme Court, and all other officers of the United States, whose appointments are not herein otherwise provided for, and which shall be established by law: but the Congress may by law vest the appointment of such inferior officers, as they think proper, in the President alone, in the courts of law, or in the heads of departments.

3. The President shall have power to fill up all vacancies that may happen during the recess of the Senate, by granting commissions which shall expire at the end of their next session.

SECTION 3. He shall from time to time give to the Congress information of the state of the Union, and recommend to their consideration such measures as he shall judge necessary and expedient; he may, on extraordinary occasions, convene both Houses, or either of them, and in case of disagreement between them with respect to the time of adjournment, he may adjourn them to such time as he shall think proper; he shall receive ambassadors and other public ministers; he shall take care that the laws be faithfully executed, and shall commission all the officers of the United States.

SECTION 4. The President, Vice President, and all civil officers of the United States, shall be removed from office on impeachment for, and conviction of, treason, bribery, or other high crimes and misdemeanors.

ARTICLE III

SECTION 1. The judicial power of the United States shall be vested in one Supreme Court, and in such inferior courts as the Congress may from time to time ordain and establish. The judges, both of the Supreme and inferior courts, shall hold their offices during good behavior, and shall, at stated times, receive for their services, a compensation, which shall not be diminished during their continuance in office.

SECTION 2. 1. The judicial power shall extend to all cases, in law and equity, arising under this Constitution, the laws of the United States, and treaties made, or which shall be made, under their authority; — to all cases affecting ambassadors, other public ministers and consuls; — to all cases of admiralty and maritime jurisdiction; — to controversies to which the United States shall be a party; — to controversies between two or more States; — between a State and citizens of another State;[1] — between citizens of different States; — between citizens of the same State claiming lands under grants of different States, and between a State, or the citizens thereof, and foreign States, citizens or subjects.

2. In all cases affecting ambassadors, other public ministers and consuls, and those in which a State shall be party, the Supreme Court shall have original jurisdiction. In all the other cases before mentioned, the Supreme Court shall have appellate jurisdiction, both as to law and to fact, with such exceptions, and under such regulations as the Congress shall make.

3. The trial of all crimes, except in cases of impeachment, shall be by jury; and such trial shall be held in the State where the said crimes shall have been committed; but when not committed within any State, the trial shall be at such place or places as the Congress may by law have directed.

SECTION 3. 1. Treason against the United States shall consist only in levying war against them, or in adhering to their enemies,

---

[1] See the 11th Amendment.

giving them aid and comfort. No person shall be convicted of treason unless on the testimony of two witnesses to the same overt act, or on confession in open court.

2. The Congress shall have power to declare the punishment of treason, but no attainder of treason shall work corruption of blood, or forfeiture except during the life of the person attained.

ARTICLE IV

SECTION 1. Full faith and credit shall be given in each State to the public acts, records, and judicial proceedings of every other State. And the Congress may by general laws prescribe the manner in which such acts, records and proceedings shall be proved, and the effect thereof.

SECTION 2. 1. The citizens of each State shall be entitled to all privileges and immunities of citizens in the several States.[1]

2. A person charged in any State with treason, felony, or other crime, who shall flee from justice, and be found in another State, shall on demand of the executive authority of the State from which he fled, be delivered up to be removed to the State having jurisdiction of the crime.

3. No person held to service or labor in one State under the laws thereof, escaping into another, shall, in consequence of any law or regulation therein, be discharged from such service or labor, but shall be delivered up on claim of the party to whom such service or labor may be due.[2]

SECTION 3. 1. New States may be admitted by the Congress into this Union; but no new State shall be formed or erected within the jurisdiction of any other State; nor any State be formed by the junction of two or more States, or parts of States, without the consent of the legislatures of the States concerned as well as of the Congress.

2. The Congress shall have power to dispose of and make all needful rules and regulations respecting the territory or other property belonging to the United States; and nothing in this Constitution shall be so construed as to prejudice any claims of the United States, or of any particular State.

[1] See the 14th Amendment, Sec. 1.
[2] See the 13th Amendment.

SECTION 4. The United States shall guarantee to every State in this Union a republican form of government, and shall protect each of them against invasion; and on application of the legislature, or of the executive (when the legislature cannot be convened) against domestic violence.

ARTICLE V

The Congress, whenever two thirds of both Houses shall deem it necessary, shall propose amendments to this Constitution, or, on the application of the legislatures of two thirds of the several States, shall call a convention for proposing amendments, which in either case, shall be valid to all intents and purposes, as part of this Constitution when ratified by the legislatures of three fourths of the several States, or by conventions in three fourths thereof, as the one or the other mode of ratification may be proposed by the Congress; Provided that no amendment which may be made prior to the year one thousand eight hundred and eight shall in any manner affect the first and fourth clauses in the ninth section of the first article; and that no State, without its consent, shall be deprived of its equal suffrage in the Senate.

ARTICLE VI

1. All debts contracted and engagements entered into, before the adoption of this Constitution, shall be as valid against the United States under this Constitution, as under the Confederation.[1]

2. This Constitution, and the laws of the United States which shall be made in pursuance thereof; and all treaties made, or which shall be made, under the authority of the United States, shall be the supreme law of the land; and the Judges in every State shall be bound thereby, anything in the Constitution or laws of any State to the contrary notwithstanding.

3. The senators and representatives before mentioned, and the members of the several State legislatures, and all executive and judicial officers, both of the United States and of the several States, shall be bound by oath or affirmation to support this Constitution; but no religious test shall ever be required as a qualification to any office or public trust under the United States.

---

[1] See the 14th Amendment, Sec. 4.

ARTICLE VII

The ratification of the conventions of nine States shall be sufficient for the establishment of this Constitution between the States so ratifying the same.

Done in Convention by the unanimous consent of the States present the seventeenth day of September in the year of our Lord one thousand seven hundred and eighty-seven, and of the independence of the United States of America the twelfth. In witness whereof we have hereunto subscribed our names.   [Names omitted]

Articles in addition to, and amendment of, the Constitution of the United States of America, proposed by Congress, and ratified by the legislatures of the several States pursuant to the fifth article of the original Constitution.

AMENDMENTS

First Ten Amendments passed by Congress Sept. 25, 1789.
Ratified by three-fourths of the States December 15, 1791.

ARTICLE I

Congress shall make no law respecting an establishment of religion, or prohibiting the free exercise thereof; or abridging the freedom of speech, or of the press; or the right of the people peaceably to assemble, and to petition the government for a redress of grievances.

ARTICLE II

A well regulated militia, being necessary to the security of a free State, the right of the people to keep and bear arms, shall not be infringed.

ARTICLE III

No soldier shall, in time of peace be quartered in any house, without the consent of the owner, nor in time of war, but in a manner to be prescribed by law.

ARTICLE IV

The right of the people to be secure in their persons, houses, papers, and effects, against unreasonable searches and seizures, shall not be violated, and no warrants shall issue, but upon probable cause, supported by oath or affirmation, and particularly describing the place to be searched, and the persons or things to be seized.

ARTICLE V

No person shall be held to answer for a capital, or otherwise infamous crime, unless on a presentment or indictment of a grand jury, except in cases arising in the land or naval forces, or in the militia, when in actual service in time of war or public danger; nor shall any person be subject for the same offense to be twice put in jeopardy of life or limb; nor shall be compelled in any criminal case to be a witness against himself, nor be deprived of life, liberty, or property, without due process of law; nor shall private property be taken for public use without just compensation.

ARTICLE VI

In all criminal prosecutions, the accused shall enjoy the right to a speedy and public trial, by an impartial jury of the State and district wherein the crime shall have been committed, which district shall have been previously ascertained by law, and to be informed of the nature and cause of the accusation; to be confronted with the witnesses against him; to have compulsory process for obtaining witnesses in his favor, and to have the assistance of counsel for his defense.

ARTICLE VII

In suits at common law, where the value in controversy shall exceed twenty dollars, the right of trial by jury shall be preserved, and no fact tried by a jury shall be otherwise reëxamined in any court of the United States, than according to the rules of the common law.

ARTICLE VIII

Excessive bail shall not be required, nor excessive fines imposed, nor cruel and unusual punishments inflicted.

ARTICLE IX

The enumeration in the Constitution of certain rights shall not be construed to deny or disparage others retained by the people.

ARTICLE X

The powers not delegated to the United States by the Constitution, nor prohibited by it to the States, are reserved to the States respectively, or to the people.

ARTICLE XI

Passed by Congress March 5, 1794. Ratified January 8, 1798.

The judicial power of the United States shall not be construed to extend to any suit in law or equity, commenced or prosecuted against one of the United States by citizens of another State, or by citizens or subjects of any foreign State.

ARTICLE XII

Passed by Congress December 12, 1803. Ratified September 25, 1804.

The electors shall meet in their respective States, and vote by ballot for President and Vice President, one of whom, at least, shall not be an inhabitant of the same State with themselves; they shall name in their ballots the person voted for as President, and in distinct ballots, the person voted for as Vice President, and they shall make distinct lists of all persons voted for as President and of all persons voted for as Vice President, and of the number of votes for each, which lists they shall sign and certify, and transmit sealed to the seat of the government of the United States, directed to the President of the Senate; — The President of the Senate shall, in the presence of the Senate and House of Representatives, open all the certificates and the votes shall then be counted; — The person having the greatest number of votes for President, shall be the President, if such number be a majority of the whole number of electors appointed; and if no person have such majority, then from the persons having the highest numbers not exceeding three on the list of those voted for as President, the House of Representatives shall choose immediately, by ballot, the President. But in choosing the President, the votes shall be taken by States, the representation from each State having one vote; a quorum for this purpose shall consist of a member or members from two thirds of the States, and a majority of all the States shall be necessary to a choice. And if the House of Representatives shall not choose a President whenever the right of choice shall devolve upon them, before the fourth day of March next following, then the Vice President shall act as President, as in the case of the death or other constitutional disability of the President. The person having the greatest number of votes as Vice President shall be the Vice President, if such number be a majority of the whole number of electors appointed, and if no person have a majority, then from the two highest numbers on the list, the Senate shall choose the Vice President; a quorum for the purpose shall consist of two thirds of the whole number of Senators, and a majority of the whole number shall be necessary to a choice. But no person constitutionally ineligible to the office of President shall be eligible to that of Vice President of the United States.

ARTICLE XIII

Passed by Congress February 1, 1865. Ratified December 18, 1865.

SECTION 1. Neither slavery nor involuntary servitude, except as punishment for crime whereof the party shall have been duly convicted, shall exist within the United States, or any place subject to their jurisdiction.

SECTION 2. Congress shall have power to enforce this article by appropriate legislation.

ARTICLE XIV

Passed by Congress June 16, 1866. Ratified July 23, 1868.

SECTION 1. All persons born or naturalized in the United States, and subject to the jurisdiction thereof, are citizens of the United States and of the State wherein they reside. No State shall make or enforce any law which shall abridge the privileges or immunities of citizens of the United States; nor shall any State deprive any person of life, liberty, or property, without due process of law; nor deny to any person within its jurisdiction the equal protection of the laws.

SECTION 2. Representatives shall be apportioned among the several States according to their respective numbers, counting the whole number of persons in each State, excluding Indians not taxed. But when the right to vote at any election for the choice of electors for President and Vice President of the United States, representatives in Congress, the executive and judicial officers of a State, or the members of the legislature thereof, is denied to any of the male inhabitants of such State, being twenty-one years of age, and citizens of the United States, or in any way abridged, except for participation in rebellion, or other crime, the basis of representation therein shall be reduced in the proportion which the number of such male citizens shall bear to the whole number of male citizens twenty-one years of age in such State.

SECTION 3. No person shall be a senator or representative in Congress, or elector of President and Vice President, or hold any office, civil or military, under the United States, or under any State, who having previously taken an oath, as a member of Congress, or as an officer of the United States, or as a member of any State legislature, or as an executive or judicial officer of any State, to support the Constitution of the United States, shall have engaged in insurrection or rebellion against the same, or given aid or comfort to the enemies thereof. But Congress may by a vote of two thirds of each House, remove such disability.

SECTION 4. The validity of the public debt of the United States, authorized by law, including debts incurred for payment of pensions and bounties for services in suppressing insurrection or rebellion, shall not be questioned. But neither the United States nor any State shall assume or pay any debt or obligation incurred in aid of insurrection or rebellion against the United States, or any claim for the loss or emancipation of any slave; but all such debts, obligations, and claims shall be held illegal and void.

SECTION 5. The Congress shall have power to enforce, by appropriate legislation, the provisions of this article.

ARTICLE XV
Passed by Congress February 27, 1869. Ratified March 30, 1870.

SECTION 1. The right of citizens of the United States to vote shall not be denied or abridged by the United States or by any State on account of race, color, or previous condition of servitude.

SECTION 2. The Congress shall have power to enforce this article by appropriate legislation.

ARTICLE XVI
Passed by Congress July 12, 1909. Ratified February 25, 1913.

The Congress shall have power to lay and collect taxes on incomes, from whatever source derived, without apportionment among the several States, and without regard to any census or enumeration.

ARTICLE XVII
Passed by Congress May 16, 1912. Ratified May 31, 1913.

The Senate of the United States shall be composed of two senators from each state, elected by the people thereof, for six years; and each senator shall have one vote. The electors in each State shall have the qualifications requisite for electors of the most numerous branch of the State legislature.

When vacancies happen in the representation of any State in the Senate, the executive authority of such State shall issue writs of election to fill such vacancies: *Provided,* That the legislature of any State may empower the executive thereof to make temporary appointments until the people fill the vacancies by election as the legislature may direct.

This amendment shall not be so construed as to affect the election or term of any senator chosen before it becomes valid as part of the Constitution.

ARTICLE XVIII
Passed by Congress December 17, 1917. Ratified January 29, 1919.

After one year from the ratification of this article, the manufacture, sale, or transportation of intoxicating liquors within, the importation thereof into, or the exportation thereof from the United States and all territory subject to the jurisdiction thereof for beverage purposes is hereby prohibited.

The Congress and the several States shall have concurrent power to enforce this article by appropriate legislation.

This article shall be inoperative unless it shall have been ratified as an amendment to the Constitution by the legislatures of the several States, as provided in the Constitution, within seven years from the date of the submission hereof to the states by Congress.

ARTICLE XIX
Passed by Congress June 5, 1919. Ratified August 26, 1920.

The right of citizens of the United States to vote shall not be denied or abridged by the United States or by any State on account of sex.

The Congress shall have power by appropriate legislation to enforce the provisions of this article.

ARTICLE XX
Passed by Congress March 3, 1932. Ratified January 23, 1933.

Section 1. The terms of the President and Vice President shall end at noon on the 20th day of January, and the terms of Senators and Representatives at noon on the 3d day of January, of the years in which such terms would have ended if this article had not been ratified; and the terms of their successors shall then begin.

Section 2. The Congress shall assemble at least once in every year, and such meeting shall begin at noon on the 3d day of January, unless they shall by law appoint a different day.

SECTION 3. If, at the time fixed for the beginning of the term of the President, the President-elect shall have died, the Vice President-elect shall become President. If a President shall not have been chosen before the time fixed for the beginning of his term, or if the President-elect shall have failed to qualify, then the Vice President-elect shall act as President until a President shall have qualified; and the Congress may by law provide for the case wherein neither a President-elect nor a Vice President-elect shall have qualified, declaring who shall then act as President, or the manner in which one who is to act shall be selected, and such person shall act accordingly until a President or Vice President shall have qualified.

SECTION 4. The Congress may by law provide for the case of the death of any of the persons from whom the House of Representatives may choose a President whenever the right of choice shall have devolved upon them, and for the case of the death of any of the persons from whom the Senate may choose a Vice President whenever the right of choice shall have devolved upon them.

SECTION 5. Sections 1 and 2 shall take effect on the 15th day of October following the ratification of this article.

SECTION 6. This article shall be inoperative unless it shall have been ratified as an amendment to the Constitution by the legislatures of three-fourths of the several States within seven years from the date of its submission.

ARTICLE XXI
Passed by Congress February 20, 1933. Ratified December 5, 1933.

SECTION 1. The Eighteenth Article of amendment to the Constitution of the United States is hereby repealed.

SECTION 2. The transportation or importation into any State, Territory, or possession of the United States for delivery or use therein of intoxicating liquors in violation of the laws thereof, is hereby prohibited.

SECTION 3. This article shall be inoperative unless it shall have been ratified as an amendment to the Constitution by conventions in the several States, as provided in the Constitution, within seven years from the date of the submission thereof to the States by the Congress.

ARTICLE XXII
Passed by Congress March 12, 1947. Ratified February 26, 1951.

No person shall be elected to the office of the President more than twice, and no person who has held the office of President, or acted as President, for more than two years of a term to which some other person was elected President shall be elected to the office of the President more than once.

But this article shall not apply to any person holding the office of President when this article was proposed by the Congress, and shall not prevent any person who may be holding the office of President, or acting as President, during the term within which this article becomes operative from holding the office of President or acting as President during the remainder of such term.

This article shall be inoperative unless it shall have been ratified as an amendment to the Constitution by the legislatures of three-fourths of the several states within seven years from the date of its submission to the states by the Congress.

ARTICLE XXIII
Passed by Congress June 16, 1960. Ratified March 29, 1961.

SECTION 1. The District constituting the seat of Government of the United States shall appoint in such manner as the Congress may direct:

A number of electors of President and Vice President equal to the whole number of Senators and Representatives in Congress to which the District would be entitled if it were a State, but in no event more than the least populous state; they shall be in addition to those appointed by the states, but shall be considered, for the purpose of the election of President and Vice President, to be electors appointed by a state; and they shall meet in the District and perform such duties as provided by the twelfth article of amendment.

SECTION 2. The Congress shall have power to enforce this article by appropriate legislation.

ARTICLE XXIV
Passed by Congress August 27, 1962. Ratified January 23, 1964.

SECTION 1. The right of citizens of the United States to vote in any primary or other election for President or Vice President, for electors for President or Vice President, or for Senator or Representative in Congress, shall not be denied or abridged by the United States or any State by reason of failure to pay any poll tax or other tax.

SECTION 2. The Congress shall have the power to enforce this article by appropriate legislation.

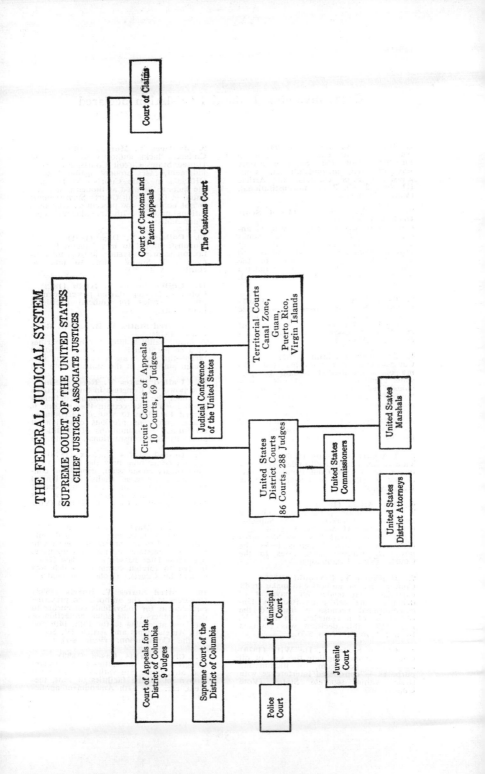

THE FEDERAL JUDICIAL SYSTEM

SUPREME COURT OF THE UNITED STATES
CHIEF JUSTICE, 8 ASSOCIATE JUSTICES

Court of Claims

Court of Customs and Patent Appeals

The Customs Court

Circuit Courts of Appeals
10 Courts, 69 Judges

Judicial Conference
of the United States

Territorial Courts
Canal Zone,
Guam,
Puerto Rico,
Virgin Islands

United States
District Courts
86 Courts, 288 Judges

United States
District Attorneys

United States
Commissioners

United States
Marshals

Court of Appeals for the
District of Columbia
9 Judges

Supreme Court of the
District of Columbia

Municipal Court

Police Court

Juvenile Court

Cases involving Federal Legislation declared Unconstitutional by the Supreme Court

1. Marbury V. Madison (1803)
An attempt to enlarge the original jurisdiction of the Supreme Court was declared unconstitutional. Congressional Acts contrary to Article III, Sec. 2, Cl. 2 are unconstitutional. (Vote Unanimous)

2. Scott V. Sandford (Dred Scott Decision) (1857)
Citizenship denied negro whose ancestors were brought to United States as slaves. The Constitution does not provide Congress with the power to abolish slavery in territories of the United States. (This decision invalidated by ratification of 13th Amendment). (Vote 6-2)

3. Gordon V. United States (1865)
Congress has no power to authorize a court to express an opinion in a case where the court is deprived of the "finality essential to judicial decisions." (Vote 8-2)

4. Ex Parte Garland (1867)
Congressional Act requiring the taking of a specified test oath by persons applying for, or attorneys previously admitted to, the bar of the Supreme Court was declared an *ex post facto* law. Applied in this case to a Confederate officeholder, the Act was declared a bill of attainder and an unwarranted interference with the President's pardoning power. (Vote 5-4)

5. Reichart V. Felps (1868)
Title to lands confirmed under Authority of an Act of the Continental Congress cannot be changed by Congress. (Vote Unanimous)

6. The Alicia (1869)
The Constitution defines the appellate and original jurisdiction of the Supreme Court (Article II, Sec. 2). In prize cases the Supreme Court has appellate jurisdiction only, and Congress lacks the power to transfer such cases to the Court. (Vote Unanimous)

7. Hepburn V. Griswold (1870)
Congress has no authority to make credit currency legal tender for payment of debts existing before its issuance. Unconstitutional because it impaired the obligation of a contract. (In Knox V. Lee, 1871, this decision was reversed by a 5-4 vote). (Vote 5-3)

8. United States V. De Witt (1870)
Congress cannot regulate the sale of oil made from petroleum, for illuminating purposes — considered interference with trade within separate States. (Vote Unanimous)

9. Justices V. Murray (1870)
Congress lacks authority to remove to United States Circuit Courts, after final judgment, cases brought against Federal Officials in State Courts—the law and the facts to be tried as though case originated in the Circuit Court. Such removal is not common law procedure. Unconstitutional under the 7th Amendment. (Vote Unanimous)

10. Collector V. Day (1871)
Unconstitutional to levy Federal income tax on salaries of state judges—interference with States' rights to maintain courts. (Vote 8-1)

11. United States V. Klein (1872)
Congress, lacking judicial powers, cannot prescribe rules for judicial decisions. (Vote 7-2)

12. United States V. B. and O. Railroad (1873)
A municipality holding taxable securities of a corporation is exempt from Federal taxes—the city being a part of the sovereign authority of the State. (Vote 7-2)

13. United States V. Reese (1876)
The power of Congress in State elections is, under the 15th Amendment, definitely limited—to make certain that no one is denied the right to vote on account of "race, color, or previous condition of servitude." Assumption of additional authority is unconstitutional. (Vote 7-2)

14. United States V. Fox (1878)
An act concerning only the State at the time of its commission, cannot be considered an offense against the United States by reason of a later independent act. (This entire Bankruptcy Law was later repealed by Congress (1878).) (Vote Unanimous)

15. Trade Mark Cases (1879)
Trade mark laws may be passed only with regard to the power of Congress to regulate interstate and foreign commerce. (Congress later passed a new law (1881) limited to foreign commerce which was upheld by Court). (Vote Unanimous)

16. United States V. Harris (1883)
Congress lacks the authority to prescribe punishment for individuals conspiring to deprive others of the equal protection of the laws according to the 13th, 14th and 15th Amendments and Article IV, Sec. 2 of the Constitution. (Vote 8-1)

17. Civil Rights Cases (1883)
Congress lacks the authority to declare that all persons are entitled to an equal enjoyment of the facilities of inns, theaters, etc. The 14th Amendment applies

only to State action; the 13th Amendment applies only to slavery and involuntary servitude. (Vote 8-1)

18. Boyd V. United States (1886)
Act of Congress requiring the production of a person's private papers or the giving of testimony against himself in an attempt to prove a crime against the United States is unconstitutional. (See 4th and 5th Amendments). (Vote 7-2)

19. Baldwin V. Franks (1887)
Unconstitutional on same grounds as United States V. Harris, No. 16. (Vote 7-1)

20. Callan V. Wilson (1888)
Congress cannot deprive persons accused of crime, the right of trial by jury as provided in Article III, Sec. 2 of the Constitution. It is not sufficient that jury trial be provided on appeals. (Vote Unanimous)

21. Counselman V. Hitchcock (1892)
A person need not be a witness against himself in any judicial proceeding even though Congress provides that such evidence shall not be used against him in any Court of the United States. (See 5th Amendment). (Vote Unanimous)

22. Monongahela Navigation Co. V. United States (1893)
As provided in the 5th Amendment, Congress cannot take private property without just compensation. Determination of "just compensation" is a judicial not legislative function. (Vote Unanimous)

23. Pollack V. Farmers' Loan and Trust Co. (1895)
Federal taxes on personal property and the income therefrom are direct taxes which can only be levied in "proportion to the census." (Congress was later given the power to levy income taxes by adoption of the 16th Amendment). (Vote 5-4)

24. Wong Wing V. United States (1896)
Under the 5th and 6th Amendments, the right to a grand jury indictment and trial by jury cannot be denied an alien charged with crime in the United States. (Vote Unanimous)

25. Kirby V. United States (1899)
Involved violation of 6th Amendment entitling an accused person to be confronted with the witnesses against him. (Criminal Code Act, 1909, repealed entire act). (Vote 6-2)

26. Jones V. Meehan (1899)
The construction of treaties is the peculiar province of the Judiciary; and, except in cases purely political, Congress has no constitutional power to settle the rights under a treaty, or to affect titles already granted by the treaty itself. (Vote Unanimous)

27. Fairbanks V. United States (1901)
Federal tax on export bills of lading unconstitutional (Article I, Sec. 9 prohibits tax on exports from any State). (Vote 5-4)

28. James V. Bowman (1903)
Action against an individual interfering with citizens' right to vote cannot be taken by the Federal Government. (15th Amendment provides the jurisdiction of the Federal Government over States, not individuals). (Vote 6-2)

29. Matter of Heff (1905)
An Act of Congress (1897) prohibiting the sale of intoxicating liquors to Indians allotted land was declared unconstitutional. The Court held that allottees under the provisions of the General Allotment Act were declared citizens and thus entitled to all the rights, privileges, etc. (This decision was later reversed by the Court, United States V. Nice, 1916). (Vote 8-1)

30. Rasmussen V. United States (1905)
The section in the Alaska Code (1900) providing that six persons should constitute a legal jury in trials for misdemeanors was declared unconstitutional. Alaska being incorporated into the United States, the Court held that persons accused of crime must be tried by a common law jury (12) as guaranteed under the 6th Amendment. (Vote Unanimous)

31. Hodges V. United States (1906)
Court ruled that interference with right of contract on account of race or color is not violation of 13th Amendment, not being "slavery or involuntary servitude." (Vote 7-2)

32. The Employer's Liability Case (1908)
An Act of Congress making interstate carriers liable for injuries to employees was declared unconstitutional. Because the terms of the law applied also to persons not engaged in interstate commerce, Congress had exceeded its authority. (A later Act, 1908 confined to interstate commerce was upheld). (Vote 5-4)

33. Adair V. United States (1908)
Congress lacks authority to make it a criminal offense for employers (interstate carriers) to discharge employees solely because of membership in a labor union. (Entire act involved in this case was repealed, 1913). (Vote 6-2)

34. Keller V. United States (1909)
The section of an act making it a felony to "harbor . . . for prostitution or for any other immoral purpose, any alien woman or girl within three years after she shall have entered the United States" was declared unconstitutional on the grounds that such regulations were not within the power of Congress under the immigration clause. (Act of Feb. 5, 1917 superseded nearly all previous immigration laws). (Vote 6-3)

35. United States V. Evans (1909)
The prosecution cannot appeal a verdict rendered by a jury in favor of a defendant in a criminal case. (Vote Unanimous)

36. Muskrat V. United States (1911)
An Act designed to obtain advance opinions on the validity of legislation was declared unconstitutional. The Court's power is limited to cases arising under the laws (Article III, Sec. 2). (Vote Unanimous)

37. Coyle V. Oklahoma (1911)
Under Article IV, Sec. 3, new States were admitted to the Union on an equal basis with other States and Congress lacks authority to interfere with strictly internal affairs. (Removal of State Capitol in Oklahoma). (Vote 7-2)

38. Choate V. Trapp (1912)
Indians' vested right to tax exemption under the provisions of the Curtis Act is protected by the 5th Amendment and may not be disturbed by Congress. (Vote Unanimous)

39. Butts V. Merchant's Transportation Co. (1913)
Without changing the original intention implied in the Act, it was impossible to separate the sections of the Civil Rights Act, March 1, 1875, which were constitutional, so the Court declared the entire Act invalid. (Vote Unanimous)

40. United States V. Hvoslef (1915)
Taxing groups who charter ships is actually a tax on the goods carried (exports) and therefore unconstitutional. (Vote Unanimous)

41. Thames & Mersey Ins. Co. V. United States (1915)
Marine insurance being necessary to export trade cannot be taxed under the Constitution. (Vote Unanimous)

42. Hammer V. Dagenhart (1918)
The regulation of hours and child labor are subject only to State authority, and thus Congress exceeded its power in prohibiting interstate shipments of goods produced by children under 14 years of age. (Vote 5-4)

43. Eisner V. Macomber (1920)
The 16th Amendment does not give Congress the power to levy income taxes on dividends from stocks. The Court ruled that taxing stock dividends was a tax on property which is a direct tax invalidated in Article I, Sec. 2, 9. (Vote 5-4)

44. Knickerbocker Ice Co. V. Stewart (1920)
Congress cannot delegate its legislative power by applying the rights and remedies of State Workmen's Compensation laws to maritime commerce. See Constitution Article I, Sec. 8. (Vote 5-4)

45. Evans V. Gore (1920)
The incomes of Federal Judges are not taxable under Article III, Sec. 1 of the Constitution which provides that compensation of Judges shall not be diminished during term of office. (Vote 7-2)

46. United States V. L. Cohen Grocery Co. (1921)
An Act making it unlawful for a person to charge unjust or unreasonable rates, etc., was held unconstitutional under the 6th Amendment—"the accused . . . shall be informed of the nature and cause of the accusation." (Vote 6-2)

47. Newberry V. United States (1921)
The Corrupt Practices Acts limiting expenditures of candidates for the United States Senate was held not to apply to primary elections. The power of Congress is limited to Article I, Sec. 4. (Vote 5-4)

48. United States V. Moreland (1922)
Prosecuted upon information rather than on indictment, a six months' workhouse sentence is an infamous punishment and a violation of the 5th Amendment. (Vote 5-3)

49. Bailey V. Drexel Furniture Co. (1922)
The entire Child Labor Tax Act was declared unconstitutional because it was obviously a penalty rather than a tax—and it violated the 10th Amendment which reserves certain powers to States. (Vote 8-1)

50. Hill V. Wallace (1922)
Tax on grain involved in sales for future delivery held invalid. Interference with authority of the State. (Vote Unanimous)

51. Lipke V. Lederer (1922)
Violation of the 5th Amendment (due process of law clause) for Congress to impose tax as a penalty on taxable goods. (Vote 7-2)

52. Adkins V. Children's Hospital (1923)
An Act to fix minimum wages in the District of Columbia held violation of 5th Amendment (due process of law clause). (Vote 5-3)

53. Keller V. Potomac Elec. Power Co. (1923)
Congress lacks the authority to either directly or by appeals confer legislative or administrative jurisdiction on the Supreme Court. (Vote Unanimous)

54. Spalding Bros. V. Edwards (1923)
Violation of Article I, Sec. 9, forbidding a tax on articles exported from a State. (Vote Unanimous)

55. Washington V. Dawson (1924)
Same grounds as Knickerbocker Ice Co. V. Stewart. See Case 44. (Vote 7-2)

56. Small V. American Sugar Refining Co. (1925)
See Lipke V. Lederer, Case 51. (Vote Unanimous)

57. Trusler V. Crooks (1926)
See Case 50. (Vote Unanimous)

58. Myers V. United States (1926)
The portion of the Tenure of Office Act (1867) providing that the President must secure the Senate's consent for removal of executive officers appointed by him was held unconstitutional. (Vote 6-3)

59. Nichols V. Coolidge (1927)
Violation of 5th Amendment (due process of law clause) to require, for purposes of estate taxation, that the value of property transferred before the Act's passage, be included in the decedent's gross estate. (Vote Unanimous)

60. Untermeyer V. Anderson (1928)
In taxing gifts which were consummated prior to the gift tax law, Congress violates 5th Amendment (due process of law clause). (Vote 6-3)

61. National Life Insurance Co. V. United States (1928)
Congress, through Federal Income Tax Laws, cannot levy taxes on income derived from state and municipal bonds. (Vote 6-3)

62. Indian Motorcycle Co. V. United States (1931)
Interferes with the instrumentalities, means and operations whereby the States exert the governmental powers belonging to them. Thus the sale of motorcycles to a State agency is not subject to taxation by the United States. (Vote 7-2)

63. Burnet V. Coronado Oil and Gas Co. (1932)
Tax Acts which "in terms include the character of income in question" may not constitutionally be given effect as against income from leases of public lands which have been granted to a State for maintenance of public schools. (Vote 5-4)

64. Heiner V. Donnan (1932)
Congress may include in a death tax, transfers made in contemplation of death, but may not attempt to create a conclusive presumption of such intent, without actualities. Such provisions may not be upheld as a gift tax because it would be contrary to the expressed intent, and would be a violation of the 5th Amendment. (Vote 6-2)

65. Booth V. United States (1934)
It is a contradiction in terms to assert that one who has retired in accordance with the statute may continue to function as a Federal judge and yet not hold the office of judge. The constitutional prohibition against diminution of salary of judges must be construed as referring to salary payable at date of appointment, irrespective of any intermediate increase. (Vote Unanimous)

66. Panama Refining Co. V. Ryan (1935) "Hot Oil Case"
Section 9c of Title I (N.I.R.A. Act, 1933) held unconstitutional. Congress cannot delegate its legislative power (e.g., prohibiting shipments in interstate commerce) to the President. (Vote 8-1)

67. Railroad Retirement Board V. Alton R. R. (1935)
The Railroad Retirement Act of 1934 was declared unconstitutional because it deprived railroads of property without due process of law and was an improper exercise of power by Congress over interstate commerce. (Vote 5-4)

68. Schechter V. United States (1935)
Section 3 of Title I (N.I.R.A. Act, 1933) declared unconstitutional on the grounds that (a) Congress lacks authority to delegate its powers to the President, (b) the codes attempted to regulate transactions within a state which lay outside the power of Congress, and (c) certain provisions were contrary to the due process of law clause. (Vote Unanimous)

69. Louisville Joint Stock Land Bank V. Radford (1935)
Frazier-Lemke Farm Mortgage Act, June, 1934, violated 5th Amendment (due process of law clause) by taking property without just compensation. (Vote Unanimous)

70. United States V. Constantine (1935)
"Where in addition to the normal and ordinary tax fixed by law an additional sum is collected by reason of conduct of the taxpayer violative of the law, and this additional sum is grossly disproportionate to the amount of the normal tax, the conclusion must be that the purpose is to impose a penalty as a deterrent and punishment of unlawful conduct." The only support for such penalty was the 18th Amendment (repealed December, 1933). (Vote 6-3)

71. Hopkins Federal Savings and Loan Assn. V. Cleary (1935)
Constitutes an infringement of State sovereignty under the 10th Amendment to the extent that it permits the conversion of state associations into Federal ones in contravention of the laws of their creation. (Vote Unanimous)

72. United States V. William M. Butler et al. Receivers of Hoosac Mills Inc. (1935)
The Agricultural Adjustment Act was held to be an invasion of the rights of States to regulate local activities. "At best it is a scheme for purchasing with Federal Funds submission to Federal Regulation of a subject reserved to States." (Vote 6-3)

73. Rickert Rice Mills Inc. V. Fontenot (1936)
The "A.A.A. processing tax" under the Amendatory Act of 1935 "still lacks the quality of a true tax." It remains for effectuating the regulation of agricultural production, a matter not within the powers of Congress. (Vote Unanimous)

74. Carter V. Carter Coal Co. (1936)
The Guffey Coal Act violates the due process clause by delegating to stated majorities of coal producers and miners power to regulate minimum hours of labor of the minority. The price fixing provisions cannot be separated from the

labor provisions, and therefore must fall with them, so that no decision as to their constitutionality as such is necessary. (Vote 5–4)

75. C. L. Ashton, et al. V. Cameron County Water Improvement District (1936)
In voiding the Municipal Bankruptcy Law the Court ruled: "Like the power of taxation, the bankruptcy power of Congress is limited by the doctrine of non-interference with State sovereignty." (Vote 5–4)

76. Tot V. United States (1943)
Federal Firearms Act, section (f), establishing a presumption of guilt based on a prior conviction and present possession of a firearm, held to violate the test of due process under the 5th Amendment. (Vote 8–0)

77. United States V. Lovett (1946)
Urgent Deficiency Appropriation Act of 1943, section 304 providing that no salary should be paid to certain named federal employees out of moneys appropriated, held to violate Article I, Sec. 9, Cl. 3, forbidding enactment of bill of attainder or *ex post facto* law. (Vote 8–1)

78. United States V. Cardiff (1952)
Federal Food, Drug and Cosmetic Act of 1938, section 301(f), prohibiting the refusal to permit entry or inspection of premises by federal officers held void for vagueness and as violative of the due process clause of the 5th Amendment. (Vote 8–1)

79. Toth V. Quarles (1955)
Article 3(a) of the Uniform Code of Military Justice subjecting civilian ex-servicemen to court martial for crime committed while in military service held to violate Article III, Sec. 2, and the 5th and 6th Amendments. (Vote 6–3)

80. Reid V. Covert (1957)
Insofar as Article 2(11) of the Uniform Code of Military Justice subjects civilian dependents accompanying members of the armed forces overseas in time of peace to trial, in capital cases, by court martial, it is violative of Article III, Sec. 2, and the 5th and 6th Amendments. (Vote 6–2)

81. Trop V. Dulles (1958)
Provision of Aliens and Nationality Code derived from the Nationality Act of 1940, as amended, that citizenship shall be lost upon conviction by court martial and dishonorable discharge for deserting the armed services in time of war, held invalid as imposing a cruel and unusual punishment barred by the 8th Amend-

ment and not authorized by the war powers conferred by Article I, Sec. 8, Cl. 11–14. (Vote 5–4)

82. McElroy V. United States (1960)
Insofar as Article 2(11) of the Uniform Code of Military Justice, subjecting civilians accompanying the armed forces to trial by court martial, is invoked in time of peace for the trial of noncapital offenses by employees of the armed forces who have not been inducted or who have not voluntarily enlisted therein, it is violative of the 6th Amendment. (Vote 5–4)

83. Kinsella V. United States (1960)
Insofar as Article 2(11) of the Uniform Code of Military Justice is invoked in time of peace for trial by court martial of noncapital offenses committed by civilian dependents accompanying members of the armed forces overseas, it is violative of Article III, Sec. 2, and the 5th and 6th Amendments. (Vote 7–2)

84. Grisham V. Hagan (1960)
Insofar as Article 2(11) of the Uniform Code of Military Justice is invoked in time of peace for the trial by court martial of a capital offense committed by a civilian employee of the armed forces overseas, it is violative of Article III, Sec. 2, and the 5th and 6th Amendments. (Vote 7–2)

85. Kennedy V. Mendoza-Martinez (1963)
Section 401(J) of the Immigration and Nationality Act of 1940, added in 1944, and section 349(a)(10) of the Immigration and Nationality Act of 1952 depriving one of citizenship, without the procedural safeguards guaranteed by the 5th and 6th Amendments, for the offense of leaving or remaining outside the country, in time of war or national emergency, to evade military service, are invalid. (Vote 5–4)

86. Schneider V. Rusk (1964)
Section 352(a)(1) of the Immigration and Nationality Act of 1952 depriving a naturalized person of citizenship for "having a continuous residence for three years" in the state of his birth or prior nationality is violative of the due process clause of the 5th Amendment. (Vote 5–3)

87. Aptheker V. Secretary of State (1964)
Subversive Activities Control Act of 1950, section 6, providing that any member of a Communist organization, which has registered or has been ordered to register, commits a crime if he attempts to obtain or use a passport, held violative of due process under the Fifth Amendment. (Vote 6–3)

JUSTICES OF THE
UNITED STATES SUPREME COURT

The Supreme Court first consisted of a Chief Justice and five Associate Justices (*Judiciary Act of 1789*). The number of Associate Justices was increased to six in 1807, to eight in 1837, and to nine in 1863. The Act of 1869 provided for a Chief Justice and eight Associate Justices. This number has remained unchanged. Their term of office is for life unless a Judge shall resign or be convicted on impeachment. It is interesting to note that in the entire history of the Supreme Court the only Justice (Samuel Chase) impeached was acquitted.

Name (Boldface denotes **Chief Justices**)	*State*	*Term*
John Jay (1745–1829)	New York	1789–1795
John Rutledge (1739–1800)	South Carolina	1789–1791
William Cushing (1732–1810)	Massachusetts	1789–1810
James Wilson (1742–1798)	Pennsylvania	1789–1798
John Blair (1732–1800)	Virginia	1789–1796
Robert H. Harrison (1745–1790)	Maryland	1789–1790
James Iredell (1751–1799)	North Carolina	1790–1799
Thomas Johnson (1732–1819)	Maryland	1791–1793
William Paterson (1745–1806)	New Jersey	1793–1806
John Rutledge (1739–1800)	South Carolina	(a) 1795
Samuel Chase (1741–1811)	Maryland	1796–1811
Oliver Ellsworth (1745–1807)	Connecticut	1796–1799
Bushrod Washington (1762–1829)	Virginia	1798–1829
Alfred Moore (1755–1810)	North Carolina	1799–1804
John Marshall (1755–1835)	Virginia	1801–1835
William Johnson (1771–1834)	South Carolina	1804–1834
Brockholst Livingston (1757–1823	New York	1806–1823
Thomas Todd (1765–1826)	Kentucky	1807–1826
Joseph Story (1779–1845)	Massachusetts	1811–1845
Gabriel Duval (1752–1844)	Maryland	1812–1835
Smith Thompson (1768–1843)	New York	1823–1843
Robert Trimble (1777–1828)	Kentucky	1826–1828
John McLean (1785–1861)	Ohio	1829–1861

(a) Senate rejected his appointment Dec. 15, 1795.

Name	State	Term
Henry Baldwin (1780–1844)	Pennsylvania	1830–1844
James M. Wayne (1790–1867)	Georgia	1835–1867
Roger B. Taney (1777–1864)	Maryland	1836–1864
Philip P. Barbour (1783–1841)	Virginia	1836–1841
John Catron (1786–1865)	Tennessee	1837–1865
John McKinley (1780–1852)	Alabama	1837–1852
Peter V. Daniel (1784–1860)	Virginia	1841–1860
Samuel Nelson (1792–1873)	New York	1845–1872
Levi Woodbury (1789–1851)	New Hampshire	1845–1851
Robert C. Grier (1794–1870)	Pennsylvania	1846–1870
Benj. R. Curtis (1809–1874)	Massachusetts	1851–1857
John A. Campbell (1811–1889)	Alabama	1853–1861
Nathan Clifford (1803–1881)	Maine	1858–1881
Noah H. Swayne (1804–1884)	Ohio	1862–1881
Samuel F. Miller (1816–1890)	Iowa	1862–1890
David Davis (1815–1886)	Illinois	1862–1877
Stephen J. Field (1816–1899)	California	1863–1897
Salmon P. Chase (1808–1873)	Ohio	1864–1873
William Strong (1808–1895)	Pennsylvania	1870–1880
Joseph P. Bradley (1813–1892)	New Jersey	1870–1892
Ward Hunt (1810–1886)	New York	1873–1882
Morrison R. Waite (1816–1888)	Ohio	1874–1888
John M. Harlan (1833–1911)	Kentucky	1877–1911
William B. Woods (1824–1887)	Georgia	1881–1887
Stanley Matthews (1824–1889)	Ohio	1881–1889
Horace Gray (1828–1902)	Massachusetts	1882–1902
Samuel Blatchford (1820–1893)	New York	1882–1893
Lucius Q.C. Lamar (1825–1893)	Mississippi	1888–1893
Melville W. Fuller (1833–1910)	Illinois	1888–1910
David J. Brewer (1837–1910)	Kansas	1890–1910
Henry B. Brown (1836–1913)	Michigan	1891–1906
George Shiras, Jr., (1832–1924)	Pennsylvania	1892–1903
Howell E. Jackson (1832–1895)	Tennessee	1893–1895
Edward D. White (1845–1921)	Louisiana	1894–1910
Rufus W. Peckham (1838–1909)	New York	1896–1909
Joseph McKenna (1843–1926)	California	1898–1925
Oliver W. Holmes (1841–1935)	Massachusetts	1902–1932
William R. Day (1849–1923)	Ohio	1903–1922
William H. Moody (1853–1917)	Massachusetts ·	1906–1910
Horace H. Lurton (1844–1914)	Tennessee	1910–1914
Charles E. Hughes (1862–1948)	New York	1910–1916
Willis Van Devanter (1859–1941)	Wyoming	1911–1937
Joseph R. Lamar (1857–1916)	Georgia	1911–1916
Edward D. White (1845–1921)	Louisiana	1910–1921
Mahlon Pitney (1858–1924)	New Jersey	1912–1922

Name	State	Term
James C. McReynolds (1862–1846)	Tennessee	1914–1941
Louis D. Brandeis (1856–1941)	Massachusetts	1916–1939
John H. Clarke (1857–1945)	Ohio	1916–1922
William H. Taft (1857–1930)	Connecticut	1921–1930
George Sutherland (1862–1942)	Utah	1922–1938
Pierce Butler (1866–1939)	Minnesota	1922–1939
Edward T. Sanford (1865–1930)	Tennessee	1923–1930
Harlan F. Stone (1872–1946)	New York	1925–1941
Charles E. Hughes (1862–1948)	New York	1930–1941
Owen J. Roberts (1875–1955)	Pennsylvania	1930–1945
Benjamin N. Cardozo (1870–1938)	New York	1932–1938
Hugo L. Black (1886–	Alabama	1937–
Stanley F. Reed (1884–	Kentucky	1938–1957
Felix Frankfurter (1882–1965)	Massachusetts	1939–1962
William O. Douglas (1898–	Connecticut	1939–
Frank Murphy (1890–1949)	Michigan	1940–1949
Harlan F. Stone (1872–1946)	New York	1941–1946
James F. Byrnes (1879–	South Carolina	(b) 1941–1942
Robert H. Jackson (1892–1954)	New York	1941–1954
Wiley B. Rutledge (1894–1949)	Iowa	1943–1949
Harold H. Burton (1888–1964)	Ohio	1945–1958
Fred M. Vinson (1890–1953)	Kentucky	1946–1953
Tom C. Clark (1899–	Texas	1949–
Sherman Minton (1890–1965)	Indiana	1949–1956
Earl Warren (1891–	California	1953–
John Marshall Harlan (1899–	New York	1955–
William J. Brennan, Jr. (1906–	New Jersey	1956–
Charles E. Whittaker (1901–	Missouri	1957–1962
Potter Stewart (1915–	Ohio	1958–
Byron R. White (1917–	Colorado	1962–
Arthur J. Goldberg (1908–	Illinois	(c) 1962–1965
Abe Fortas (1910–	Tennesee	1965–

(b) Resigned October, 1942 to assume chairmanship of Economic Stabilization Board.

(c) Resigned July, 1965 to assume post of United States Ambassador to the United Nations.

QUALIFICATIONS AND POWERS OF GOVERNMENT OFFICIALS

THE PRESIDENT (Term 4 years)

Qualifications.

A natural born citizen. Fourteen years a resident in the United States. At least 35 years of age.

Powers and Duties.

Execution of all laws. Makes treaties with advice and consent of Senate. Appoints ambassadors to foreign countries, Judges of the Supreme Court and of the inferior federal courts, and about 17,000 other officers of the national government. Recommends measures to Congress. Convenes extraordinary sessions of Congress. Has veto power over legislation except it be repassed by a two-thirds majority. Commander-in-Chief of the armed forces. Takes office January 20th. Limited to two elective terms and a maximum of ten years in office.

Salary and Allowances.

Salary of $100,000 per year. Special taxable allowance of $50,000 for White House and other expenses, plus a maximum of $40,000 (non-taxable) for travel and entertainment.

VICE PRESIDENT (Term 4 years)

Qualifications.

Same as for President.

Powers and Duties.

Presiding Officer of the Senate — votes only in case of tie. Office of little importance except for the possibility of succeeding to the Presidency (eight of thirty-six Presidents have died in office).

Salary and Allowances.

Salary of $45,000 per year plus $10,000 per year for expenses.

PARTY ORGANIZATION
UNITED STATES HOUSE OF REPRESENTATIVES

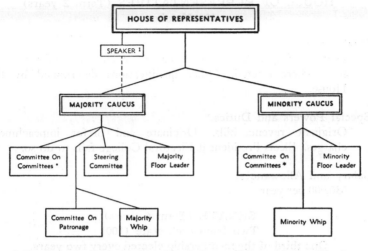

HOUSE OF REPRESENTATIVES

SPEAKER [1]

MAJORITY CAUCUS

Committee On Committees *

Steering Committee

Majority Floor Leader

Committee On Patronage

Majority Whip

MINORITY CAUCUS

Committee On Committees *

Minority Floor Leader

Minority Whip

1. The speaker is in fact the choice of the Majority Caucus, though formally selected by a vote of the whole House.

* Members of the Ways and Means Committee in Democratic Organization.

PARTY ORGANIZATION
UNITED STATES SENATE

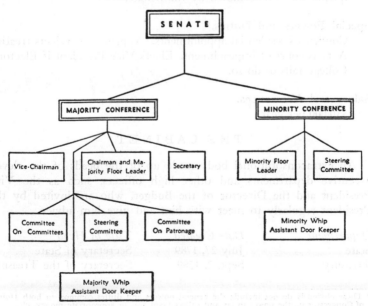

SENATE

MAJORITY CONFERENCE

Vice-Chairman

Chairman and Majority Floor Leader

Secretary

Committee On Committees

Steering Committee

Committee On Patronage

Majority Whip Assistant Door Keeper

MINORITY CONFERENCE

Minority Floor Leader

Steering Committee

Minority Whip Assistant Door Keeper

HOUSE OF REPRESENTATIVES (Term 2 years)
435 Members

Qualifications.
> 25 years of age. An American citizen seven years. Inhabitant of state where elected. Other qualifications determined by the House.

Special Powers and Duties.*
> Originate revenue bills. Originate and prefer impeachment charges. Elects President if Electoral College fails to do so.

Salary and Allowances.
> $30,000 per year.

SENATE (Term 6 years)
Two from each state (100)
One third of the membership elected every two years.

Qualifications.
> Not less than 30 years of age. At least nine years a citizen. Must be an inhabitant of the state from which he is elected. Other qualifications determined by the Senate.

Special Powers and Duties.*
> Confirms Presidential appointments. Approves or rejects treaties. Acts as court of impeachment. Elects Vice President if Electoral College fails to do so.

Salary and Allowances.
> $30,000 per year.

THE CABINET

An extraconstitutional body made up of the heads of the eleven executive departments and other high officers, such as the Vice President and the Director of the Budget, who are invited by the President regularly to meet with him and give him advice.

Department	Date Created	Title of Head
State	July 27, 1789	Secretary of State
Treasury	Sept. 2, 1789	Secretary of the Treasury

---

* These obviously do not include the general powers and duties common to both Houses of Congress, e.g., the power to lay and collect taxes and to appropriate money, etc.

Post Office	March 9, 1829	Postmaster General
Interior	March 3, 1849	Secretary of the Interior
Justice	June 22, 1870	Attorney General
Agriculture	Feb. 9, 1889	Secretary of Agriculture
Commerce	March 4, 1913	Secretary of Commerce
Labor	March 4, 1913	Secretary of Labor
Defense	July 26, 1947	Secretary of Defense
Health, Education and Welfare	April 11, 1953	Secretary of Health, Education and Welfare
Housing and Urban Development	Sept. 9, 1965	Secretary of Housing and Urban Development

A single Department of Commerce and Labor had been established on February 14, 1903, but in 1913 two separate departments were created. The Department of the Army (formerly the War Department, established in 1789) and the Department of the Navy (established in 1798) were organized under the Defense Department by the same 1947 legislation which created the Defense Department and made its Secretary a cabinet member. The Secretaries of the Army and Navy no longer have cabinet status.

SUCCESSION TO THE PRESIDENCY

The Vice President is the constitutional successor to the President. To provide for succession in case of the death, resignation, or disability of both the President and the Vice President, a law of Congress in 1792 put the President pro tempore of the Senate and the Speaker of the House, in that order, next in line of succession. In 1886 this law was repealed and the succession devolved upon the heads of the executive departments in the order of their creation, except that the Secretary of the Treasury was placed ahead of the Secretary of War and the Attorney General was raised from seventh to fourth place. In 1947 Congress again changed the order of succession. After the Vice President, it is: the Speaker of the House, the President pro tempore of the Senate, the Secretaries of State, the Treasury, and Defense, the Attorney General, the Postmaster General, and the Secretaries of the Interior, Agriculture, Commerce, and Labor. The Secretary of Health, Education, and Welfare and the Secretary of Housing and Urban Development are not included in this order because these offices were created after the 1947 succession law.

PRESIDENTS OF THE UNITED STATES

No.	Name	Native State	Party	Term
1	George Washington *(1732-1799)*	Va.	Federalist	1789-1797
2	John Adams *(1735-1826)*	Mass.	Federalist	1797-1801
3	Thomas Jefferson *(1743-1826)*	Va.	Rep.-Dem.	1801-1809
4	James Madison *(1751-1836)*	Va.	Rep.-Dem.	1809-1817
5	James Monroe *(1758-1831)*	Va.	Rep.-Dem.	1817-1825
6	John Quincy Adams *(1767-1848)*	Mass.	Rep.-Dem.	1825-1829
7	Andrew Jackson *(1767-1845)*	S. C.	Democrat	1829-1837
8	Martin Van Buren *(1782-1862)*	N. Y.	Democrat	1837-1841
9	William Henry Harrison *(1773-1841)*	Va.	Whig	1841
10	John Tyler *(1790-1862)*	Va.	Democrat	1841-1845
11	James Knox Polk *(1795-1849)*	N. C.	Democrat	1845-1849
12	Zachary Taylor *(1784-1850)*	Va.	Whig	1849-1850
13	Millard Fillmore *(1800-1874)*	N. Y.	Whig	1850-1853
14	Franklin Pierce *(1804-1869)*	N. H.	Democrat	1853-1857
15	James Buchanan *(1791-1868)*	Pa.	Democrat	1857-1861
16	Abraham Lincoln *(1809-1865)*	Ky.	Republican	1861-1865
17	Andrew Johnson *(1808-1875)*	N. C.	Republican	1865-1869
18	Ulysses S. Grant *(1822-1885)*	Ohio	Republican	1869-1877
19	Rutherford B. Hayes *(1822-1893)*	Ohio	Republican	1877-1881
20	James A. Garfield *(1831-1881)*	Ohio	Republican	1881
21	Chester A. Arthur *(1830-1886)*	Vt.	Republican	1881-1885
22	Grover Cleveland *(1837-1908)*	N. J.	Democrat	1885-1889
23	Benjamin Harrison *(1833-1901)*	Ohio	Republican	1889-1893
24	Grover Cleveland *(1837-1908)*	N. J.	Democrat	1893-1897
25	William McKinley *(1843-1901)*	Ohio	Republican	1897-1901
26	Theodore Roosevelt *(1858-1919)*	N. Y.	Republican	1901-1909
27	William H. Taft *(1857-1930)*	Ohio	Republican	1909-1913
28	Woodrow Wilson *(1856-1924)*	Va.	Democrat	1913-1921
29	Warren G. Harding *(1865-1923)*	Ohio	Republican	1921-1923
30	Calvin Coolidge *(1872-1933)*	Vt.	Republican	1923-1929
31	Herbert C. Hoover *(1874-1964)*	Iowa	Republican	1929-1933
32	Franklin D. Roosevelt *(1882-1945)*	N. Y.	Democrat	1933-1945
33	Harry S. Truman *(1884-)*	Mo.	Democrat	1945-1953
34	Dwight D. Eisenhower *(1890-)*	Texas	Republican	1953-1961
35	John F. Kennedy *(1917-1963)*	Mass.	Democrat	1961-1963
36	Lyndon B. Johnson *(1908-)*	Texas	Democrat	1963-

ENTRANCE OF STATES INTO UNION

Original thirteen states indicated by italics.

State	Settled	Area Sq. Mi.	Entered Union
Alabama	1702	51,998	1819
Alaska	1783	586,400	1958
Arizona	1580	113,956	1912
Arkansas	1785	53,335	1836
California	1769	158,297	1850
Colorado	1858	103,948	1876
Connecticut	1635	4,965	1788
Delaware	1638	2,370	1787
Florida	1565	58,666	1845
Georgia	1733	59,265	1788
Hawaii	c500	6,449	1959
Idaho	1842	83,354	1890
Illinois	1720	56,043	1818
Indiana	1733	36,045	1816
Iowa	1788	55,586	1846
Kansas	1727	81,774	1861
Kentucky	1775	40,181	1792
Louisiana	1699	45,409	1812
Maine	1624	29,895	1820
Maryland	1634	9,941	1788
Massachusetts	1620	8,039	1788
Michigan	1668	57,480	1837
Minnesota	1805	80,858	1858
Mississippi	1699	46,362	1817
Missouri	1764	68,727	1821
Montana	1809	146,131	1889
Nebraska	1847	76,808	1867
Nevada	1850	110,690	1864
New Hampshire	1623	9,031	1788
New Jersey	1664	7,514	1787
New Mexico	1537	122,503	1912
New York	1614	47,654	1788

North Carolina	1650	48,740	1789
North Dakota	1780	70,183	1889
Ohio	1788	40,740	1803
Oklahoma	1889	69,414	1907
Oregon	1838	95,607	1859
Pennsylvania	1682	45,126	1787
Rhode Island	1636	1,067	1790
South Carolina	1670	30,495	1788
South Dakota	1794	76,868	1889
Tennessee	1757	41,687	1796
Texas	1686	262,398	1845
Utah	1847	82,184	1896
Vermont	1724	9,124	1791
Virginia	1607	40,262	1788
Washington	1845	66,836	1889
West Virginia	1727	24,022	1863
Wisconsin	1670	55,256	1848
Wyoming	1834	97,548	1890

TERRITORIES AND DEPENDENCIES

		Area Sq. Mi.
	Acquired	
American Samoa	1899 — U.S. claims recognized by Germany and Great Britain in treaty	76
Canal Zone	1904 — Leased in perpetuity from Panama	553
Guam	1899 — ceded to U.S. by Spain	206
Puerto Rico	1899 — ceded to U.S. by Spain	3,435
Virgin Islands	1917 — purchased from Denmark	133
Wake, Midway, and other Pacific Islands		42

SELECTED REFERENCES

Adams, Randolph G. *Political Ideas of the American Revolution* (1958).
Anderson, W., *et al. Government in the Fifty States* (1960).
Appleby, P. H. *Policy and Administration* (1949).
Babcock, R. S. *State and Local Government and Politics*, rev. ed. (1962).
Beard, Charles A. *Economic Interpretation of the Constitution of the United States* (1935).
Brown, Robert E. *Charles Beard and the Constitution* (1956).
Bone, H. A. *American Politics and the Party System*, 3rd ed. (1965).
Brandeis, L. D. *The Social and Economic Views of Mr. Justice Brandeis* (1930).
Campbell, A. *The American Voter* (1960).
Cardozo, B. N. *The Nature of the Judicial Process* (1921).
Carr, R. K., *et al. American Democracy in Theory and Practice* (1963).
Carr, R. K. *Supreme Court and Judicial Review* (1942).
Corwin, E. S. *Doctrine of Judicial Review* (1914).
————. *John Marshall and the Constitution* (1936).
————. *The Presidency: Office and Power* (1957).
Corwin, E. S., and Peltason, J. W. *Understanding the Constitution*, 3rd ed. (1964).
Council of State Governments. *Book of the States* (Published Annually).
Cushman, R. E. *Leading Constitutional Decisions* (1963).
Farrand, Max. *Framing of the Constitution of the United States* (1913).
Ferguson, J. H., and McHenry, D. E. *The American System of Government.* 8th ed. (1965).
Galloway, George B. *History of the House of Representatives* (1962).
Hamilton, Alexander, *et al. The Federalist Papers.*
Holcombe, Arthur N. *Our More Perfect Union: From 18th Century Principles to 20th Century Practice* (1950).
Hoover Commission. *Report on the Organization of the Executive Branch of Government* (1949).
Jensen, Merrill. *The New Nation* (1950).
Jacobsen, G. A., and Lipman, M. H. *Political Science*, College Outline Series (1956).
Johnson, C. O. *American National Government* (1964).
————. *American State and Local Government* (1965).
Key, V. O. *Politics, Parties, and Pressure Groups*, 5th ed. (1964).
Koenig, Louis W. *Chief Executive* (1964).
Krout, John A. *United States to 1865*, College Outline Series (1962).
————. *United States since 1865*, College Outline Series (1960).

Mason, Alpheus T., and Beaney, W. M. *American Constitutional Law*, 3rd ed. (1964).

McLaughlin, Andrew C. *Constitutional History of the United States* (1935).

Ogg, F. A., and Ray, P. O. *Essentials of American Government* (1964).

Pritchett, Charles H. *The American Constitution* (1959).

Randall, J. G. *Constitutional Problems under Lincoln* (1951).

Rossiter, Clinton. *Political Thought of the American Revolution* (1963).

Sayre, W. S. *American Government*, College Outline Series (1962).

Smelser, M. *American Colonial and Revolutionary History*, College Outline Series (1950).

————. *American History at a Glance*, Everyday Handbook Series (1961).

Smith, E. C., and Zurcher, A. J. *Dictionary of American Politics*, Everyday Handbook Series (1955).

Solberg, Winton U., ed. *Federal Convention and the Formation of the Union of the American States* (1958).

Swisher, Carl B. *American Constitutional Development* (1954).

Syrett, H. C. *American Historical Documents*, College Outline Series (1960).

Tresolini, Rocco J. *American Constitutional Law*, 2nd ed. (1965).

United States Government Organization Manual (Published Annually).

Wilson, W. *Constitutional Government in the United States* (1908).

Young, Alford. *Ratification of the Constitution* (1965).

Zimmerman, J. *State and Local Government*, College Outline Series (1962).